Don't Go to Work on Mondays

Don't Go to Work on Mondays

Don't Punch a Shark on the Nose,
Never Shower in a Thunderstorm and
Other Amazing Facts About You and Your Life

Anahad O'Connor

Michael O'Mara Books Limited

First published in Great Britain in 2007 by
Michael O'Mara Books Limited
9 Lion Yard
Tremadoc Road
London SW4 7NQ

First published in the United States of America in 2007 as *Never Shower in a Thunderstorm* by Times Books, Henry Holt and Company, LLC, 175 Fifth Avenue New York, NY 10010

A CIP catalogue for this book is available from the British Library.

Permission to reprint Celia Fleischer's recipe for chicken soup on p. 137 granted by Stephen I. Rennard et al. The recipe originally appeared in Barbara O. Rennard, Ronald F. Ertl, et al., 'Chicken Soup Inhibits Neutrophil Chemotaxis *In Vitro*', *Chest,* vol. 118, 2000, pp. 1150–1157.

ISBN: 978-1-84317-271-0

1 3 5 7 9 10 8 6 4 2

www.mombooks.com

Typeset in the UK by K DESIGN, Winscombe, Somerset
Printed and bound in Great Britain by Clays Ltd, St Ives plc

Papers used by Michael O'Mara Books Limited are natural, recyclable products made from wood grown in sustainable forests. The manufacturing processes conform to the environmental regulations of the country of origin.

To my mother, Karen,
for her boundless love and support,
and to my very first editor at *The New York Times*,
the late John Wilson,
whom I miss dearly.

Contents

Introduction

In the modern world it seems there are far more health-related questions and answers than ever before as academic studies, copious self-help books, and the Internet all teem with a multitude of symptoms and treatments. Some of these explanations and cures carry weight and some are just plain wrong. But how do you set about sifting the true from the false?

Don't Go to Work on Mondays does the work for you; containing answers scoured from reams of medical journals, interviews with experts, and some disciplined reconsideration of the advice handed down by previous generations. The results range from the eminently practical to the historically remarkable – such as why Britain's air strategy during World War II has meant that generations of children have been forced to eat up their carrots at dinner.

The stories also offer a window on to the extraordinary and sometimes comical lengths that scientists have gone to in order to unravel quirky and intriguing curiosities about our health. You need only consider the legions of researchers who have, in the name of science, locked people in freezers, collected nasal secretions, and forced themselves to walk around in wet clothes to find out whether catching a chill really can cause a cold. And who would have thought that teams of scientists visited nursing homes in search of lifelong knuckle crackers with arthritis of the hands, to see if parental warnings were true? Or that studies had examined family recipes to figure out whether chicken soup really can cure a cold?

So book Monday off work (you'll soon find out why), settle down and read on . . .

1
Human Nature?

The great DNA lottery

Does your DNA determine your destiny?

It used to be that scientists believed our genes were responsible for a select number of our physical features, and that was about it. We began almost as blank slates and our behaviour was determined largely by our environment, moulded over the years through stimulus and response.

It was an overly simplistic view. A better understanding of human genetics eventually showed that we don't have nearly as much control over who we are and how we behave as we think we do. A few years ago, a look at the newly-mapped human genome showed that there were genes that could help determine whether a person grew up to be fat, an alcoholic or a thrill-seeking hang-glider. There is even a shyness gene.

Suddenly, it seemed that the truth of the matter was some-where in the middle: many of our traits are both inherited and environmentally responsive. It's not nature versus nurture, but nurture complementing nature. Our genes set us on a path at birth and guide us, but ultimately our experiences lead us to decide how far we go and where we stop along the way.

That being said, it is human nature to wonder to what extent our genes control the course of our lives, and how. Part of it is that we want to know what makes us tick and why we are who we are. Another part of it is our desire to gain some inkling of our fate. If someone told you they could let you in on the time and the date of your death, as the old saying goes, wouldn't you want to know?

Does cutting your hair make it grow back thicker?

For some reason, people of all ages consider this question of hair-cutting one of biblical import, more urgent than questions about diseases and more pressing than the fear-inducing old wives' tales that mothers have been spreading for centuries.

Part of the reason might be that cutting or trimming hair on various body parts is something we all have to deal with at some point – sometimes hair we wanted to be thick and sometimes, unfortunately, hair we really didn't want at all. And almost all of us grew up convinced that the claim was true. I have to confess that I was one of those children who would occasionally steal his father's shaving cream and razor, slip into the bathroom, and shave away non-existent facial hair, hoping it would turn into a thick moustache. For my sisters and other women, on the other hand, the notion that hair grows back darker and thicker is a nuisance; a reason to spend money on waxes and trips to the salon.

But despite what millions of people think, trimming or waxing hair on any part of your body isn't going to speed its rate of growth, make it thicker, or change its texture. When this myth was born is not exactly clear, but it has been around in scientific literature for well over half a century. The first studies to show that cutting hair doesn't stimulate growth were performed in the 1920s, and many more have been carried out since then. All had the same results: the length, texture and coarseness of your hair are determined by genetics and hormone levels, not by how often you shave, pluck or Nair it away.

But according to dermatologists, there are several reasons why trimming your hair on a regular basis creates the illusion that it is growing back faster and thicker.

Many people – myself included – start shaving at an early age, while their hair is still lightly coloured or not growing at the rate it's destined to reach. Since hair is darker and rougher at its roots, removing the tips gives the appearance of coarser hair. And the bristly stubble that emerges after shaving is also more noticeable than the same amount of growth in hair that's already long. Plus, many people don't realize that the hair that we see above the surface of the scalp is already dead, which means there's no way that cutting it can affect the living section that we don't see below the scalp. No matter how often you trim your hair, it will always grow back at a rate of about half an inch each month.

So, men and boys who shave their faces won't speed up the growth of their eagerly-awaited lumberjack beard, and women who get peach fuzz removed from their faces – with the strange exception of one girl I knew at school – won't sprout real moustaches.

Is male pattern baldness inherited from your mother's side of the family tree?

Before we answer this question, we should probably take a look at what seems like the much bigger issue here: why do bald men get such a bad press?

Ever since the Middle Ages, people have considered baldness a disease, like bad skin or leprosy. Hundreds of years ago, baldness was seen as a sign of mental illness; the thinking apparently went that a frail mind couldn't support a full head of hair, much like dry soil can't support a plant. Then there were those who blamed a thin head of hair on sexual frustration, a belief that stemmed from observations of eunuchs, who have no desire for sex. People who have no testicles, it seems, never go bald.

All these ugly connotations have driven men to go to extraordinary and sometimes ridiculous lengths to hold on to their hair, spending millions of pounds on pills, creams and other dubious cures.

It was only five decades ago that researchers came up with a credible theory: that baldness has something to do with the X chromosome, which men inherit from their mothers. That prompted hordes of men who noticed their hair vanishing prematurely to lay the blame squarely on their mothers – or, more specifically, on their mother's father.

Most scientists, meanwhile, said that it couldn't be true. All the blame and resentment that maternal grandfathers had been getting from their balding grandsons was misplaced, they said, because baldness is caused by high levels of testosterone, hence the tendency for castrated men (and women in general) to avoid going bald.

We finally know that both sides were right. With sophisticated genetic testing, in 2005 scientists were able to pinpoint a gene variation that turns up frequently in bald men. It was identified in a study in the *American Journal of Human Genetics* that looked at balding men from ninety-five different families, each of which had at least two male siblings with early hair loss. The culprit, a variant of the androgen receptor gene, sits on the X chromosome, which men get from their mothers (Y comes from the father). It turns out that this variant increases the effects of testosterone and other male hormones, called androgens, which have been linked to baldness for ages. Scientists say this gene variant may be the 'cardinal prerequisite' for premature balding in a lot of men, but it's also possible that a number of genes and factors could be involved to a lesser extent, including genes that cause premature hair loss on a father's side.

All of which means at least two things. If you're a guy and your grandfather on your mother's side has little or no hair, start preparing yourself for the likelihood that you may go bald. Number two, if you're already bald and you're reading this while you're standing on your head, you can stand up now.

Do babies tend to look more like their fathers?

It's one of the first questions to cross a new parent's mind: does the baby look like me? Any proud parent wants to see his or her own features in a son's or daughter's face, but Dad really does have a stronger claim on the newest family nose.

For new fathers, there may have been a time when seeing a familiar feature in that face was more a matter of necessity than vanity. A new mother can always be sure that a child belongs to her; that much we know. But long before the advent of paternity tests, a new father could never be certain that a child was actually his. If the basic goal of reproduction is to pass on genes, then why, from an evolutionary standpoint, would a male invest the time, energy and resources needed to raise a child of dubious paternity, when he could easily move on and father a new one?

Scientists have argued for years that evolutionary pressures would have made it beneficial for a child to resemble his or her father. In the event that a father believed that a child was not his, the likelihood of him abandoning it or even killing it outright would be great. Look no further than the fact that infanticide is widely prevalent among chimpanzees and others of our relatives in the animal kingdom for some evidence. In addition, scientists who support this theory also point out that even among humans today, children are far more likely to be abused or killed by step-parents than their natural parents.

But there is also reason to suspect that the reverse theory might be true: couldn't it also be in a child's interest to conceal its identity? If children unambiguously resembled their fathers, then a prospective father could be certain not only when a child was his, but also when a child was not. For the child, bearing a strong resemblance to one particular man could heighten the odds of being abandoned almost as much as being accepted.

Yet, studies have tended to find the opposite. One from 1995 in the journal *Nature*, for example, put the question to the test by having 122 people try to match pictures of children they didn't know – at one year, ten years, and twenty years – with photos of their mothers and fathers. The group members correctly paired about half of the infants with their fathers, but their success rate was much lower matching the infants with their mothers. And matching the twenty-year-olds with either parent proved to be just as tough.

Another paper from 2003 echoed those findings, although this time the team that carried out the study took a more unusual approach. The researchers took head shots of a group of people and morphed them with photos of baby faces without the subjects' knowledge. When they presented the group with the digitally created faces, the men were more likely to indicate that they would adopt or spend time with the babies – male and female – who had been rendered with more of their facial characteristics. The women in the study, meanwhile, showed no preference at all for the children with their features.

As with most evolutionary theories, the case is not closed, perhaps because there are too many holes. Think back thousands of years, before there were mirrors, windows and cameras. Besides the occasional reflection in a body of water, how often would our predecessors have had the opportunity to see what they looked like?

Probably not often. So even if a baby did slightly resemble its father, how would he know? How would the father know what he looked like himself?

No one can say for sure. And now we have daytime television to clear up any cases of paternity uncertainty.

Do identical twins have identical fingerprints?

They share personality traits, interests and habits. They come from the same fertilized egg and share the same genetic blueprint.

To a standard DNA test, they are indistinguishable. But any forensics expert will tell you that there is at least one sure-fire way to tell identical twins apart: despite what most people think, they do not have matching fingerprints.

Like physical appearance and personality, fingerprints are largely shaped by a person's DNA and by a variety of environmental forces. Genetics help determine the general patterns on a fingertip – arches, loops, whorls. An individual finger can have just one of these patterns or a mix of them.

But there are plenty of other factors that play unique roles, too. While a foetus is developing, the ridges along the patterns on the fingers are altered by bone growth, pressures within the womb, and even contact with amniotic fluid. This, according to Gary W. Jones, a former fingerprint specialist with the Federal Bureau of Investigation, is what causes the unique ridge characteristics in every person's fingers.

Identical twins often have similar arrangements of patterns because of their identical genes. But they never have the same minute details. 'It's impossible for people to have identical fingerprints,' said Jones. 'The study of fingerprints has been around for about a hundred years, and in all that time, two people have never been found to have the same prints.'

The patterns on a person's fingers, palms and feet are fully formed by roughly the fifth month of pregnancy. Barring any changes brought on by severe mutilation or a skin disease, the patterns stay the same for life. But even with severe traumatic damage, they change very little.

John Dillinger, the notorious Depression-era bank robber, famously tried to elude the authorities by altering his face and obliterating the skin on his fingertips with acid. It turned out to be his very last mistake. After the legendary gangster was killed, experts discerned a few of his remaining ridge patterns and had no trouble identifying him.

Are older siblings really smarter?

As the second youngest of seven brothers and sisters – four boys and three girls – I was always trying to prove myself to my older siblings. Growing up in their shadows, I had to fight to make myself stand out. If my siblings gave my mother a birthday card, I would bake her a cake. My oldest brother played hockey, so I joined a team and became captain. His best subject at school was chemistry, so I made it mine too.

Anyone who has grown up in a large family has experienced sibling rivalry in some form or another. So when I learned a few years back that there was scientific evidence that older siblings are often more intelligent, it came as a slap.

The scientific literature, it turns out, is rife with studies claiming that IQ scores and other measures of intelligence dwindle among siblings with decreasing age. It's a phenomenon caused, supposedly, by the increasing strain on parents' time, energy and resources as their families expand. Another theory holds that firstborns are more intelligent because they're surrounded mainly by adult influences in their early years, forcing them to mature faster than children who interact mostly with other infants. Seven kids certainly kept my parents busier than when they had just one and whether we were fighting, playing sports or on holiday, my siblings and I spent almost all of our time together, but how could any of that have been a detriment to my intelligence?

Thankfully, science appears to prove that the birth-order effect is more myth than reality, a theory that is illusion rather than fact. Multiple studies have debunked it. One published in 2006 analyzed data on siblings from three thousand families collected over twelve years and found that it makes no difference whether you're born first or last.

The one thing that does seem to matter is family size. Children in large families, primarily those in which the mother had her first child at a young age, end up with lower scores on intelligence tests than those in smaller ones. In studies, they only seem to have higher scores when their mothers are older. Sounds odd, until you consider that there is probably a socio-economic reason behind all this. Younger mothers are more likely to have lower incomes and less education – factors that could negatively affect their children's test scores, scientists suspect.

'A mother's age is associated with many variables that can affect the child-rearing environment,' said Dr Aaron L. Wichman, a psychologist at Ohio State University, USA, who has studied the birth-order effect. 'It's not your birth order that's important; it's your family environment and your genetics that really matter.'

So, younger siblings: hold on to your bragging rights.

Can being stressed while you're pregnant harm your child?

Most pregnant women know that whatever they eat or drink goes straight to their child. So it seems logical to think that whatever stress a pregnant woman endures will also end up affecting her baby – and very likely causing harm.

The widespread notion that stress can somehow affect a developing foetus and should be avoided at all costs may seem like a product of our modern society, where technology makes it possible to study a foetus's every blink and hiccup and women are urged to put the health of their babies above all else.

But the claim has actually been around for centuries, woven through fiction, folk tales and religious texts. In Shakespeare's *King Henry VI*, a pregnant Queen Elizabeth fights back anguish in one scene, lest, she says, 'with my sighs or tears I blast or drown King Edward's fruit.' But only in the late twentieth century have we finally been able to scientifically investigate the claim, and what studies have revealed is surprising. Extreme emotional distress and anguish can in fact slow foetal development, and perhaps even increase the risk of miscarriage – but a little stress and anxiety can also do some good.

There are no direct neural connections between a mother and her foetus, so stress has to impact a foetus somewhat indirectly, and it is thought to do so in two ways. The first is through a drop in blood flow to the foetus, which can deprive the baby of oxygen and nutrients. The other is through the passage of stress-related hormones across the placenta. Certain stress hormones like cortisol are necessary for organ growth and normal foetal development, but they can also do damage when their levels are disrupted or climb too high.

Much of the evidence that maternal stress causes long-lasting damage and behavioural problems for a child later in life comes from animal studies. Most scientists don't put too much stock in applying those studies to people, though, since the stressful situations they employ – physical restraint, prolonged exposure to very loud music – don't exactly mimic (hopefully) what humans experience in the real world.

Still, there have been a small number of studies showing that maternal grief can lead to foetal defects and slowed development. One powerful example: a study by a US team of researchers at Mount Sinai School of Medicine, New York, that looked at 187 pregnant women who either lived near the World Trade Center on 9/11 or escaped from the towers. The women who showed the most symptoms of post-traumatic stress, it turned out, gave birth to babies with the smallest head circumferences, a sign that the children suffered stunted cognitive development.

But a typical pregnant woman isn't going to experience anything nearly as traumatic. The stress most pregnant women grapple with daily is moderate and it tends to come in the form of work, family and personal problems. When a group of US researchers at the Johns Hopkins University, Baltimore, Maryland, and the National Institutes of Health recently tried to examine the long-term impact of different levels of normal stress on a foetus, they were shocked.

The study, which followed 137 healthy women with low-risk, normal pregnancies, found that those who reported relatively moderate levels of everyday stress had children who were slightly more advanced in mental and motor development at age two than their peers – a finding that contradicts a lot of assumptions from earlier animal studies.

One possibility is that cortisol at moderate levels is extremely beneficial. Another is that women who deal with a lot of day-to-day stress are also high achievers, and subsequently more likely to push their children more. Either way, one thing is clear, said Janet DiPietro, a developmental psychologist who has published widely on the subject: 'Expectant mothers shouldn't worry about worrying.'

That's a relief.

Do tall people live longer than short people?

Everyone knows that being tall has its benefits: greater social and economic prospects, an advantage in mate selection, a better shot of making it as a model. But to the list of indignities faced by shorter people, should we really add a shorter lifespan?

That's the conclusion reached by a large number of scientists, who argue, sadly for those of us south of five foot eight, that

greater height means a longer life. That finding is certainly in keeping with the 'heightism' experienced by shorter people in a society where being tall has enormous perks. Studies show that tall people are automatically considered more intelligent, more attractive and more likeable. All but five of the last forty-three American presidents were above average height and tall men are more likely to be married and to have more children than their shorter counterparts. A study in 2006 by two economists even concluded that the reason taller people make more money is because they're more intelligent. Ouch.

But the height-life span claim has more to do with historical observations than intelligence tests. Scientists have known for years that as the standard of living in a society improves – giving people greater access to nutrition – the average height and lifespan tend to go up. Widespread malnutrition and hardship, on the other hand, usually have the opposite effect.

You can see this in modern-day China, where the economy and the average height, which has increased at the rate of about an inch per decade, have grown together. Similarly, the average height in South Korea has been climbing. The average South Korean man is now several inches taller than the average man in neighbouring North Korea, where malnutrition is endemic.

As a result, many researchers have argued that greater height reflects better health, and, in turn, a longer life. For instance, one group of epidemiologists at Bristol University have shown that taller people are less likely to die of coronary heart disease, respiratory disease and stomach cancer than shorter people. Another study looked at three-thousand-year-old skeletons excavated from a site in north-east England and, after excluding the bones of children, found that the longer bones came from the remains of people who had lived longer.

But others say shorter is better. Taller people consume more calories, and more calories means quicker ageing. Men are also 8 per cent taller than women on average, and women have the upper hand when it comes to lifespan. So what to make of all this? The truth is, there probably is a slight advantage to being taller when it comes to lifespan – but to what extent is unknown. And in the end, there's only one relationship between size and mortality that people today can really do anything about: an expanding waistline lowers your life expectancy.

Do right-handed people live longer than lefties?

Look no further than the etymology of 'left' to see that lefties, who make up about 10 per cent of the population, have been slighted for centuries. In Latin, the word for left is *sinister*, while the word for right is *dexter*, related to dexterity. In French, the word for left, *gauche*, means clumsy; the word for right, *droit*, gives us the term adroit.

But the notion that lefties have a shorter lifespan stems largely from a popular 1991 study that found that their proportion in the population dwindles with age. Lefties live in a world designed for right-handers, the researchers explained, and are thus more prone to accidents and serious injuries. Lefties are more likely to suffer power-tool accidents, wrist fractures and depression.

In 1992, one psychologist, Stanley Coren, argued that these mishaps significantly shrink the average age at which lefties die. After examining thousands of death certificates, Coren suggested that lefties, on average, bite the dust about nine years earlier than their right-handed counterparts.

Was there some flaw in the research, people asked, or could it really be true that left-handed people are dealt a bad hand?

If you're a leftie, don't get down. In 2000, a researcher at Penn State University showed that there was a simple explanation for the lefty conundrum. Many elderly right-handed people started out as lefties, but were pressured into switching as children. Think of all those left-handed children in Catholic schools who had to put up with nuns standing over them, ruler in hand, forcing them to use their right hands. That practice is less common today.

Since that initial research suggesting that lefties die younger, two more studies have examined the issue, one in *The Lancet* and another in the *British Medical Journal*. The studies looked at thousands of right- and left-handed people, and both found similar lifespans.

Then again, there are some things about lefties that can't be explained so easily. For whatever reason, whether it's the

27

pressures of living in a world designed for righties, or all the talk of having shorter lifespans, lefties suffer higher rates of depression, drug abuse, allergies and schizophrenia. But lefties also have an advantage in sports like fencing and tennis, not to mention greater academic success and higher IQs. Five of the United States's last eleven presidents were lefties, even though they make up only 10 per cent of the American population.

Now if only they could find a way to be less clumsy.

Do our eyes change colour as we age?

It can bend light, bring the world into focus and, next to the human brain, may be our most complicated organ. But for many people the most intriguing feature of the human eye is simply its colour.

Can it really change for no apparent reason?

In most people, the answer is no. Eye colour fully matures in infancy and remains stable for life. But a lot of people know someone who swears that the coloured part of their eyes, called the iris, was dark blue as a child and then turned hazel or brown as they aged. I have a friend with light green eyes who says they were brown when she was a baby. I always teased her and accused her of lying. But according to studies, in a small percentage of adults, eye colour can naturally become either noticeably darker or lighter as they get older.

What determines eye colour is the pigment melanin. Eyes that have a lot of it in the connective tissue at the front of the iris, called the stroma, are darker, while those that have less tend to be lighter.

The levels of melanin generally remain the same throughout life, but a few things can change them permanently.

The first is a handful of ocular diseases like pigmentary glaucoma. Certain glaucoma medications can even cause colour changes by increasing the amount of pigment in the eye. Another condition, called heterochromia or multicoloured eyes, affects about 1 per cent of the population and is often caused by traumatic injuries. An example can be seen in musician David Bowie, who says his contrasting eye colours, hazel and light blue, resulted from a blow to his face when he was a child.

And the last and most frequent cause: our good friend, genetics. A study in 1997, for instance, looked at thousands of twins and found that 10 to 15 per cent of them had gradual changes in eye colour throughout adolescence and adulthood – which occurs at nearly identical rates in identical twins.

But what if it seemed like every morning you woke up your eyes had changed colour? As bizarre as it sounds, there are actually people who claim that their eyes shift hues from one day to the next, or even, at times, from one moment to the next, depending on their moods or their outfits.

It's a phenomenon that can occur, but it can also be a trick of the eye.

People perceive colours based on the light that bounces off objects, and some of that light – for instance, the red light from a red jacket – is going to be reflected in the eyes. In a person with black or brown eyes, the reflected colour is hard to notice. But in a person whose eyes are more pale – particularly hazel or blue – that reflected light on the iris creates the illusion that the eye has shifted colours. Clothing can have this effect, but so can a different pair of glasses or a new hair colour.

Even the mood you're in can do it. Anger and other emotions that dilate your pupils, which determine how much light reaches the back of your eyes, for example, can make your iris seem like it's a different colour.

Perhaps green-eyed envy isn't only a metaphor.

2
Sex, Sex, Sex
Aphrodisiacs and other risky business

As a science writer, you learn to expect certain questions from strangers. Meet someone at a bar and tell them you spend your days poring over studies to get answers to medical questions for a newspaper column and invariably they want to know three things.

The first is what they should eat, do and cut out of their lives to lower their odds of getting the big disease that runs in their family (the most popular one: Alzheimer's). Then they want to know the truth about something their mother told them as a child, something they never forgot, always adhered to closely, but now, as an adult, are not so sure about, time-honoured questions such as 'Can I read in the dark without hurting my eyes?' (See Chapter 8 for that one.)

Then, eventually, the comfort level goes up, and people invariably move on to their favourite topic: sex.

I'm going to make it easy for you and jump right in.

No, having sex while standing up is not considered a form of birth control. Yes, a lot of things besides swimming pools can, in fact, cause shrinkage (anger, fear, cold air). Yes, there are some women out there who can have multiple orgasms (13 per cent!). And no, a man can never run out of sperm, no matter how much time he spends alone in his room or on the Internet. And those are just a few of the ones that are printable.

It has never surprised me that misconceptions about sex are so rampant. But what *has* surprised me is that the answers that people are looking for to their questions about sex are so scarce, and the places where they can go to get them even more so. Most doctors don't have the time or the patience to answer them, and most researchers don't take questions from the general public. Besides, most people are too embarrassed even to bring them up.

But even doctors and scientists that I've interviewed while tracking down answers don't always have them, and it's often the case that even when they do, some other expert out there who is just as qualified or knowledgeable on the subject completely disagrees. Often, it takes sifting through countless studies to get to the truth.

Once you've done so, questions about sex can be split into two categories: those that can be answered with a quick yes or no, like the ones mentioned earlier, and those fuzzier ones that have been lurking around the human imagination for ages, woven into folklore, reinforced by history, and at times linked to famous icons – if not completely inspired by them. The answers are rich, layered and most of all intriguing, like an orgasmic slice of chocolate cake.

Is chocolate an aphrodisiac?

Chocolate, it can be said, is not merely a confectionery, but a powerful love potion whose reputation for inspiring amorous feelings is universally known.

At body temperature, it quickly melts on the tongue, an act that in itself can be a stimulating experience. It contains caffeine, sugar and other stimulants, and besides just tasting good, it raises the spirits and imparts a feeling of deep satisfaction.

The Aztecs, who helped introduce the cocoa bean to the world, may be the first on record to draw a link between chocolate and sexual desire. The emperor Montezuma considered it a sort of ancient Viagra, consuming it in copious amounts to fuel romantic trysts with his many wives. Legend has it that he drank fifty cups of chocolate a day.

But men are not the only ones in history who have turned to chocolate for a lift. Madame du Barry, mistress of Louis XV, and a reputed nymphomaniac, always, as a matter of course, shared a cup of chocolate with her lovers before allowing them to step one foot inside her bedroom. Then there was Madame de Pompadour, another famous – and only slightly less promiscuous – French mistress, who was known to start her days with chocolate to stimulate her desire for the king.

Nowadays, we tend to put our faith in chocolate as a catalyst of romance only when Valentine's Day rolls around. But its reputation as an aphrodisiac is no less strong. So is there anything to it?

Most scientists believe that the aphrodisiac qualities of chocolate, if any, can be ascribed to three or four chemicals. One, tryptophan, is a building block of serotonin, the brain chemical that creates feelings of pleasure, helps soothe pain and plays a role in sexual arousal. Another is theobromine, a chemical stimulant that is similar to caffeine but has a great ability to elevate mood. This is the chemical that can make a Snickers bar lethal to dogs and horses (they metabolize theobromine more slowly than humans).

Then there is phenylethylamine, which – it turns out – is released in the brain when people fall in love. Though chocolate contains phenylethylamine in small quantities, it's not clear that it's enough to produce any measurable effects on desire. One study found that levels of the chemical in the blood do not rise after people eat chocolate. Another, published in the journal *Sexual Medicine* in 2006, looked at a large sample of women and found no differences in the rates of sexual arousal among those who regularly ate one serving of chocolate a day, those who had three or more, and those who generally ate none.

How about oysters?

Perhaps no food has developed more of a reputation for romance than the oyster. Ancient cultures considered oysters reminiscent of female genitalia in both appearance and texture, leading them to believe that they imparted sexual prowess. Henry Fielding's *Tom Jones* made the sensuality of devouring oysters unforgettable, and Giacomo Casanova, the eighteenth-century Venetian, reportedly ate dozens of oysters at a time to stir arousal before his legendary assignations.

Consider Casanova's description of feasting on oysters with one of his paramours, Signorina 'M. M.', a mistress of the French Ambassador to Venice, the Abbé de Bernis, a man so kinky he would often watch Casanova and M. M. go at it from a secret hiding place. 'She offered me hers on her tongue at the same time that I put mine between her lips; there is no more lascivious and voluptuous game between two lovers, it is even comic, but comedy does no harm, for laughter is only for the happy. What a sauce that is which dresses an oyster I suck in from the mouth of the woman I love!'

In a word: steamy.

No wonder people have been trying to recreate fits of lovemaking à la Casanova for over two hundred years. Yet after all these centuries, the science behind the claim that oysters are the catalyst of passion remains murky.

Oysters are high in zinc, and a number of studies have linked zinc deficiencies to impotence and delayed sexual development. Some have found that giving zinc supplements to men who are impotent and have low levels of the mineral can boost their libidos and lead to more frequent sex. But so far no major study has shown that eating an oyster or two (or a dozen) has any direct impact on arousal in the average person.

One study, conducted by Italian researchers in 2005, came close. It found that Mediterranean mussels contained high levels of two amino acids, D-aspartic acid and N-methyl-D-aspartate, which have been shown to stimulate the release of sex hormones in animals. The study, though intriguing, had one major flaw: its findings apply only to mussels, not oysters.

But what many people fail to realize is that an aphrodisiac need not be a food, drug or scent. In fact, more often than not, the effect is psychological. Many sex researchers and experts point out that the most powerful sex organ is the brain. Often all it takes to provoke sexual arousal in someone is simply telling them that a food they're eating or a scent they're smelling is an aphrodisiac.

Oysters may be an old favourite, but there are a number of foods that can put people in the mood. Researchers in Chicago came up with a list a few years ago by exposing people to different foods and aromas while analyzing the flow of blood to their genitalia, a measure of arousal. Here, surprisingly, is what they found: for men, baked cinnamon buns had such a powerful impact on libido that they trumped the scents of a slew of various perfumes combined. Men were also strongly aroused by the scent of pumpkin pie, lavender, doughnuts, cheese pizza, buttered popcorn, vanilla and strawberries. The foods and smells that got women going more than anything else were liquorice, banana nut bread, cucumber and chocolate.

What do all these foods have in common? They may not exactly sound sexually enticing, but they can stir feelings of comfort, security and nostalgia and melt away anxiety – all of which can have a powerful aphrodisiac effect on the mind.

Does Spanish fly really exist?

It sounds like a joke or a recent invention, but Spanish fly, the emerald green beetle prized for its reputation for making people ravenously sexual, has been around for centuries. Legend has it that in Roman times Emperor Nero's troublesome wife would lace her guests' food with Spanish fly for kicks. Henry IV is said to have sworn by it, and the Marquis de Sade reportedly used it to initiate orgies.

Spanish fly comes in two forms. There's the cocktail, made with one part tequila, one part Cuarenta y Tres and a garnish of cinnamon. This drink will get you extremely drunk, but it doesn't have any special ability to make you horny. Then there's the Spanish fly aphrodisiac, which is made from the dried, crushed body of the Spanish fly beetle. It's thought to work by irritating the lining of the urethral passages, which produces an itching sensation that supposedly triggers the desire to have sex.

No study, however, has ever proven that Spanish fly has aphrodisiac qualities. And if used in anything other than small amounts, it can be toxic, causing permanent damage to the kidneys and genitals.

Don't worry, though. Most people never have much opportunity to use Spanish fly anyway. It's banned in the United States, and most of the products that are advertised as Spanish fly are nothing more than cayenne pepper in capsules.

Can a man tell if a woman is faking it?

And the Academy Award for best actress goes to . . . women everywhere for their masterful performances in the bedroom. A look at various surveys shows that between 50 and 70 per cent of all women say they have faked orgasm at one time or another, most often because they wanted to please a guy, were nervous or stressed, or, to paraphrase a line from *Seinfeld*, because it was enough already and they just wanted to get some sleep.

Surveys that ask men whether they believe they have ever been on the receiving end of a fake orgasm are much harder to come by. But my pavement-pounding observations suggest that in such a survey, the percentage of men who would admit that they've thought so would fall somewhere between 0 and 1 per cent. No man wants to believe he was unable to satisfy a lover in bed despite his best efforts. And perhaps women are simply better at faking than men are at detecting.

A lot of women seem to think that is precisely the case. One female friend sneered when I mentioned the question, saying it would end up being one of the shortest journalistic reports in history because the correct answer *obviously* consists of only one word: no.

But whatever your stance on faking the Big O, for many women – and some men, unwittingly it seems – it is a part of life. The blunt fact is that while the signs of female orgasms vary greatly from one woman to the next, there are certain features that are unmistakable and guaranteed. Women can hone their acting skills all they want, but a keen observer with enough knowledge of physiology can probably tell. Let's face it, if orgasms were so easily forged and reproduced without any flaws or weaknesses, they might not be so coveted.

According to surveys, studies and medical texts, every female orgasm is preceded by four stages. They are not unlike the stages that precede a man's orgasm. In the first stage, the clitoris becomes erect, the inner two-thirds of the vagina enlarge, and the skin around it grows darker. These are signs that blood flow to the area is increasing. In stage two, the nipples harden and the breasts become sensitive. Then there is stage three, which is all about the breathing. Breaths become faster, shorter and deeper, and in some cases almost rhythmic, as the body tries to take in more oxygen. Then, just before that all-important climactic stage, the upper body flushes; the woman's neck and her chest turn red, and her cheeks turn a pinkish hue.

This is when Mount Vesuvius is at its breaking point. What follows next are muscle spasms that ripple through the entire body, particularly in the vagina, the uterus and the pelvic floor. The first contractions are the strongest. As this is happening, a woman's thighs will shake slightly and her back will tighten and stretch uncontrollably.

Vocals are a big giveaway. Soft moans and incomplete sentences are the signs that an orgasm might be real. If a woman lets out a coherent sentence or screams so loud that she wakes up the neighbours, the chances are she's acting. During climax, the body releases oxytocin, endorphins and other pleasurable hormones that induce feelings of giddiness, warmth and relaxation. In women, this rush of hormones and emotions results in a brief high that sticks around even after the sex is over. So if a woman starts talking about shopping immediately after sex or jumps out of bed as though nothing has happened, then the chances are nothing did.

Are hormones in milk causing girls to hit puberty earlier?

Think for a second about how much milk you consume on a daily basis. Beyond the classic glass of milk that we gulp down with a meal, many of us start our mornings over a cup of coffee or tea with milk, a bowl of cereal, a yoghurt or some other dairy-based food. Then there's all the cheese and butter we have with our lunches and dinners, the ice cream we eat for dessert, and the chocolate we can't keep our hands off of during the day.

By some estimates, the average American consumes nearly seven hundred pounds of dairy products every year, making it the largest part of their diets. Americans are consuming more dairy than ever before.

So when a large study in the US in 1997 found that girls were starting puberty sooner than usual, it seemed only natural to consider the possible contribution of milk towards this trend.

The evidence was mostly anecdotal, but it seemed to be there for everyone to see. Doctors and paediatricians had been saying that more and more six- and seven-year-old girls were showing up in their offices with breasts and pubic hair. School teachers were saying that as the boys in their classes stayed physically the same from one generation to the next, the girls were sprouting womanly physiques much sooner.

Then, the 1997 study of seventeen thousand girls aged three to twelve discovered that girls were entering puberty about a year before textbooks said was normal. Black girls were developing breasts and pubic hair just before nine, and white girls were developing breasts just before nine and pubic hair at ten-and-a-half.

A substance given to cows to increase milk production, called recombinant bovine growth hormone, became a prime suspect, and almost immediately, sales of organic dairy products took off. Could the artificial growth hormone be speeding development in children?

Further studies have found no link. Instead, if girls are maturing sooner, a notion that many scientists still dispute, it may have more to do with obesity than milk.

Although recombinant bovine growth hormone is administered to dairy cows, it's not clear that the hormone actually makes its way into milk. If it did, it would probably have little impact, since in order for it to act it must be injected, not digested.

Other studies have shown that girls who are noted as developing earlier tended to have higher body-mass indexes, which can create the false impression that they have breast tissue. Consider that the findings of the early puberty study coincided with a rise in nationwide rates of obesity, and suddenly it looks as though the early puberty conclusion may have been premature.

The ironic part is that whether girls are actually reaching puberty sooner or simply gaining more weight earlier, the underlying reason remains the same: too much milk, cheese and ice cream.

Can sex trigger a heart attack?

Rumours flew in 1979 when Nelson A. Rockefeller died of a heart attack in circumstances described by his speechwriter as 'undeniably intimate'. By 'intimate', he apparently meant lying in bed with a mistress who was half his age.

But the notion that sexual activity can trigger a heart attack has been around for ages. In fact, the belief that physical exertion in the bedroom places strain on the heart prompts many people – heart patients, the elderly, obese people – to limit their activities in the sack or to abstain from sex altogether.

Their loss.

While there is certainly some truth to the claim, it's clear from research that it's largely exaggerated. Sexual activity can certainly ramp up cardiovascular activity. But it won't do any harm unless you're swinging from the chandeliers. And in fact, for most people, even those with a heart condition, it's recommended.

In 1996, a team of scientists at Harvard conducted a study of more than eight hundred heart attack survivors around the country. They found that the chance of sex causing a heart attack was about two in a million, even in subjects who had already had a previous one.

That's double the risk faced by healthy people in the two hours after sexual intercourse, but the risk is already so low to begin with that it shouldn't stop heart patients from being sexually active. Then, in 2001, a group of Swedish researchers who studied 699 heart attack survivors reported similar results, finding that the risk was extremely small, but highest among patients who were sedentary. 'While there is some truth to the mythology,' said Dr Murray Mittleman, an associate professor at Harvard Medical School and an author of the 1996 study, 'the absolute increase in risk is so small that for the vast majority of people it should be one less thing to worry about.'

Particularly if you manage to fit a few minutes of exercise into your schedule once in a while. As the amount of exercise you get on a daily basis climbs, your risk of suffering a heart attack in the sack drops. But there are things that can make your risk go up: more intense sex is one, and risky sex is another. Not risky sex as in unprotected sex, but risky as in extramarital.

The odds against you worsen when you're a former governor with political aspirations. Legend has it that on that fateful night in 1979, Rockefeller's twenty-seven-year-old mistress (and staff member) was so concerned about hiding the affair that she couldn't figure out what to do as her boss lay on the ground. She finally called an ambulance after an hour and a half. According to police reports, Rockefeller died not in his bed, but on the way to the hospital.

Will having sex before sports hinder your performance?

No one knows exactly when it started, but the idea that athletes should abstain from sex before a crucial game has been a golden rule of sports for centuries. The Roman historian Pliny the Elder was among the first to examine the link closely, but he gave it a positive spin. 'Athletes when sluggish are revitalized by lovemaking,' he wrote in AD 77.

The legendary Greek poet Homer had a different take. In a dialogue around 347 BC, he described an Olympic champion named Ikkos of Tarentum whose training regimen consisted of eating cheese, feasting on wild boar and not having sex – he believed that sex before an event could sap his strength and deplete his energy.

More than a millennium later, in the spirit of Ikkos, it has become routine for coaches in almost every sport to forbid their players from having sex before game night in order to conserve their energy and increase their levels of aggression. Boxers like Lennox Lewis and Muhammad Ali have said they would go without sex for weeks before a big fight. And Olympic swimmers and track-and-field stars have said that sex before an event can have drastic consequences: according to published reports, one Olympian, American swimmer Josh Davis, who won three gold medals at the 1996 games in Atlanta, blamed his failure to qualify for the 2004 games in Athens on the fact that he had sex with his wife on the day of his trials.

But study after scientific study – yes, there are actually scientists out there racking their brains over this one – say it's bogus. If anything, abstaining from sex before sports can only hurt your performance. In 2000, in a report in the *Clinical Journal of Sport Medicine* entitled 'Does Sex the Night Before Competition Decrease Performance?', an epidemiologist reviewed dozens of findings and established that sex between married people burns no more than fifty calories. Most people burn more energy than that taking their dog for a walk. The study also found no evidence that sex causes muscle weakness.

In fact, other studies have found that sex reduces muscle pain (particularly in women), relieves sports injuries, and puts you in a state of relaxation that can be extremely beneficial when it comes to sports that require coordination and muscle control, like golf and tennis. One study in the *Journal of Sports Medicine and Physical Fitness* even administered maths tests to professional athletes after sexual intercourse and found that it had no effect on their mental concentration.

Apparently, their test scores were just as low after sex as they were before it.

As for aggression, scientists have found that testosterone levels in both men and women climb as sexual activity increases, suggesting that more late-night rendezvous in the bedroom might lead to higher rates of aggression the next day – and enhance athletic performance.

Do bicycle seats cause impotence?

For anyone who loves a good bike ride, few things are as exciting as hopping on the saddle and climbing a few hills or flying down the side of a mountain like a rocket. Gruelling as it can be, the agony and the soreness the next day are

always worth it. And even a calm and slow-paced ride can be a thrill.

Or at least that was the case until 1997, when a urologist who studies cyclists turned the entire cycling world on its ear with his scientific assertion that there are only two types of riders – 'those who are impotent, and those who will be impotent.'

Talk about killing the excitement. A lot of people ride their bikes to stay fit, but until then few had given any serious thought to the idea that cycling could be a hazard to their sex life. As someone who once spent an entire summer biking cross-country – 60 to 120 miles a day, day in and day out – the news hit me like a ton of bricks.

To be sure, there was evidence to back it up. One study in 1998 that looked at hundreds of healthy male cyclists in their twenties and thirties found that they had a higher rate of erectile dysfunction than a group of male runners of similar age and health. The more a person rode his bike, the scientists found, the greater his risk of impotence or loss of libido. And researchers in Austria found that men who were riding their mountain bikes for a couple of days a week and who were apparently in peak physical shape still had one-third the sperm counts of a group of healthy non-cyclists.

The problem: when a man sits on a bike seat, a critical artery that runs through the perineum and delivers blood to the penis is squashed, much like a straw being flattened. It usually bounces back, but eventually it is flattened one too many times and stays that way. And it should be noted that in women, the arteries that engorge the clitoris during sex are probably affected in the same way. Although women haven't been studied as extensively, they can end up with similar damage. About 60 per cent of women who ride their bikes frequently – three to four times a week for an hour or two at a time – experience numbness, tingling and pain.

44

Traditional bike seats are so narrow that they fail to distribute weight evenly. That prompted seat manufacturers to create ergonomic saddles with splits in the back or holes in the centre, thinking that this could relieve the pressure. But it didn't really help. With smaller surface areas, the ergonomic saddles instead force some men to concentrate even more weight on the perineum. And gel saddles are no better, since the gel they contain can get mushy and form bumps in precarious areas.

So what to do? The best seats, it turns out, are those that protect the perineum by forcing you to sit back. It also helps to point the saddle downward a bit and to stand up every now and then for a couple of minutes at a time. This not only relieves pressure, but helps make you seem superior.

Can having sex while you're pregnant induce labour?

Expectant mothers whose babies are late have long been told that they can end their pregnancies the same way they began – with sex. Compare that method with running around the block a few times or drinking castor oil – two other folk beliefs – and it's no surprise that surveys of pregnant women have found sex to be the most popular option.

Clumsy though it may be, sex during pregnancy most definitely beats a lot of older methods. Pilgrims were known to strap women whose babies were late to a pole and then shake them up and down, thinking the baby would fall out.

The reasons so many people believe having sex can induce labour vary widely. Rachel on *Friends* put it bluntly while trying to coax Ross into helping her jump-start her labour: 'Just think of me as a ketchup bottle; you know, sometimes you have to bang on the end of it just to get something to come out.'

But whatever the reasons behind the claim, and despite its popularity, there is no real science to support it. According to one in-depth study in 2006, the first to examine the belief, sex in the late stages of pregnancy not only does not hasten labour and delivery, it may even do the opposite.

The study, in the American journal *Obstetrics and Gynecology*, followed ninety-three women in their third trimesters. It found that those who reported having sex in their final weeks of pregnancy – about half – delivered on average at 39.9 weeks, compared with 39.3 weeks among those who had abstained.

But that's not all. Part of the pseudo-scientific explanation for the practice is that human sperm contains small amounts of the hormone prostaglandin, which in some cases can stimulate the cervix and help start contractions. Most doctors actually administer artificial prostaglandin to help women who want to go into labour have their babies. But in the study, the women who were sexually active underwent pre-labour exams, and they showed no signs of any so-called 'ripening' effect. In the end, sex may not be a reliable method for kick-starting a labour, but unlike some other methods there's no evidence it can hurt the baby. And at least you'll burn those fifty calories or so while you're waiting for that stubborn baby to make its debut.

3
Survival of the Fittest
Is that gym membership
really worth it?

To eat well and exercise often are divine. That sums up the lifestyle message that is hammered into our heads from the time we start school.

We are told to do everything humanly possible to get our hearts pumping and our blood flowing with iron regularity, even as our technological advances make it less and less necessary to leave home, and all we want to do is hibernate. Even more galling, we are told to watch what we eat with religious zeal. But in reality, to eat healthily and stay fit is easy to say and nearly impossible to accomplish.

No surprise, then, that many people end up fooling themselves. Nearly two-thirds of people who are overweight *say* that they have healthy eating habits, but frequently eat foods that qualify as junk, and a large proportion of people who say they always exercise as often and as vigorously as they can somehow remain overweight.

We truly are locked in a struggle to stay fit, with the media and obesity experts pulling us in one direction and a culture of gluttony pulling us in the other.

As with any battle, a quick and simple way out is always tantalizing. Which is why we so easily fall prey to exercise gimmicks and diet fads: they give us hope that we can cut corners and still look good or lose weight. Besides, a world where we really did eat right and exercise every day would be an awfully boring place.

But what should we believe and what should we ignore?

Are there really foods that can make us lose weight – foods that have *negative* calories? Can you yo-yo diet and still come out on top? And what about those abs, what's the best way to get a six-pack? Then there are the fat questions. Do you really put more weight on by eating late at night, and conversely, can you burn more fat off by exercising in the morning on an empty stomach? Then finally, the question that has crossed everyone's mind at some point: when your exercise routine hits an impasse, what *really* happens to your physique? Do all those muscles simply melt to fat?

Does muscle convert to fat when you stop working out?

When summer heats up and people flock to the beach and expose their bodies, those of us whose gym memberships collected dust over the winter are often filled with dread. The once rippling six-pack and tight biceps look as though they melted away.

But while it's tempting to think that all those muscles simply turned to fat, that's not the case.

When people stop exercising and move into couch-potato mode, their muscles begin to shrink, clearing the way for adipose tissue, aka fat, to slide slowly into their place. At the same time, many people who stop exercising often continue to consume the same amount of calories they took in during their more active days, despite the fact that their energy expenditure is no longer what it once was. Plus, muscle increases your metabolic rate and allows you to burn more calories than you normally would.

All of this can create the illusion that a lean six-pack and rippling set of biceps turned to fat. But muscle and fat are really two distinct tissues that never convert to the other. The bare facts: 'What happens is that the ratio of fat to muscle has changed,' said Dr Gerard P. Varlotta, an associate professor at New York University.

But even people who refuse to hit the gym can avoid this fate. Despite what some personal trainers say, most people in decent shape can keep their muscles from shrinking through moderate activities or chores, like cleaning the house, walking the dog, even a quick walk around the house from time to time.

Sounds ridiculous? In 2005, a group of researchers at the Mayo Clinic in Minnesota, USA, reported that they had attached motion sensors to twenty people – ten who were lean and ten who were overweight – for ten straight days. The sensors showed that while the heavier subjects were prone to sitting, the lean ones spent two more hours a day standing, pacing and just generally moving around the house. At the end of the study, all that fidgeting burned a total of about 350 calories a day – or roughly thirty pounds a year.

Are you still sitting down?

Is running so bad for your knees that you should stop jogging?

As anyone who jogs regularly will tell you, a life of pounding the pavement is a sure-fire path to a lifetime of aching knees and joints.

No surprise, then, that one of the most prominent concerns for regular runners is osteoarthritis, the degenerative joint disease. It's one reason that long-time athletes who fear being saddled with achy legs abandon their trainers and switch to lower impact sports, like cycling, walking or tennis. In the worst-case scenario, it prompts people to switch to the king of all low-impact activities: staying home and watching television.

But in most cases, jogging will not only do little or no damage to your knees, it may actually end up protecting – that's right, protecting – your joints. It's a notion that's been borne out in numerous studies, which have shown that people who jog moderately a few times a week do not increase their risk of developing osteoarthritis. Compared with those who don't exercise at all, recreational runners are generally less likely to suffer from joint problems.

When problems arise, it's usually because a person has overworked a previously injured knee or joint, something that happens all the time among professional athletes and the reason they have higher rates of arthritis in their arms and legs. One study found that people who suffer joint injuries as young adults are almost twice as likely to develop osteoarthritis by the age of sixty-five as people without previous injuries.

In people with healthy joints, however, moderate exercise strengthens bones and muscles, which is the best thing you can do to ward off serious problems. Because running helps you to shed weight, in the long haul, you actually end up reducing the stress that excess pounds can place on your joints and knees. All of which means you ultimately lower your odds of developing arthritis.

A study by researchers at Stanford demonstrated this by comparing hundreds of runners to non-runners over a five-year period. Although the runners regularly experienced small aches and pains, they had fewer joint or muscle problems than the non-runners – and they spent about 33 per cent less time in the hospital, had lower blood pressure, and missed half as many work days. Another study, in the *American Journal of Sports Medicine,* looked at thirty runners who averaged more than twelve miles a week over four decades and found that their rates of arthritis in the hips, knees and ankles were no more than average. Some researchers have argued that running can delay the onset of arthritis by as much as twelve years.

What most people don't realize is that, more often than not, jogging injuries are caused by inappropriate or worn-out shoes rather than the act of running itself. Some people mistakenly wear shoes that cause their feet to turn inward too much, or overpronate, which causes backaches and knee pain, while others choose shoes that do the reverse.

So the next time you go for a jog and your legs or back start to ache, take a look at your shoes, not your regimen.

Are ab machines the best way to build a firm six-pack?

Building muscle is usually simple. If you want bigger arms, you do bicep curls. If you want stronger thighs, you do leg raises. But what if you want a lean stomach and firm set of abs?

According to a common misconception, the quickest way to burn fat around the midsection is to huff and puff on an ab machine. That notion feeds into a widespread belief that you can slim specific areas of the body – or spot reduce – by doing certain exercises.

There are plenty of people who seem to believe it: Americans, for example, spend more than $100 million on gadgets for their abdominal muscles every year.

But the truth is that, liposuction notwithstanding, spot reducing is impossible. When we gain weight, we add fat to certain sections of our bodies before adding it elsewhere, and where it goes is determined by gender and genetics. Women typically gain weight around their hips and their thighs first, while men are more likely to store fat around their midsections first, giving them that spare-tire look.

As it turns out, when we shed pounds, the weight from those areas is usually the last to go.

And keep in mind that most abdominal exercises will strengthen muscles, but have little impact on the fat deposits that sit above them. Just as doing side leg lifts won't trim fat from the hips, doing merely abdominal exercises won't burn off fat around the midsection. The best regimen for a defined midsection does not involve abdominal training alone. Better to combine dieting and plenty of cardiovascular exercise – to streamline overall body fat – with the usual abdominal workouts.

So what about all those expensive devices advertised on TV? Americans may be shelling out millions of dollars for them, but

a 2004 study by a team of researchers at Kansas State University found that they probably aren't getting their money's worth. In the experiment, a group of twenty-three male and female college students exercised with various devices – including those popular abdominal rollers and sliders – while electrodes measured the stimulation to their abdominal muscles. The electrodes showed that on average the various products elicited no greater muscle activity than traditional crunches.

In fact, two of the devices, the ab 'slide' and a type of Swiss ball called 'FitBall', caused more activity in the hip flexors than in the stomach, something the researchers ominously called 'an undesirable feature of abdominal exercises'. Simple – and free – crunches should do just fine, after a few minutes on the treadmill, of course.

Does exercising on an empty stomach burn more fat?

For most people who exercise in the morning, there is no getting around it: eat and run? Or run and eat later?

Personal trainers will tell you that eating first provides fuel for a proper workout. But one common belief is that exercising on an empty stomach forces the body to tap into its reserves, burning off calories stored as fat and providing a more efficient workout. I've always been told that exercising on an empty stomach is the quickest way to a leaner body, a way to banish all those pounds that collect around the waist.

So which camp is right?

According to researchers, there is no simple answer. One study in 1995 that examined the claim directly reported that people did burn more calories from fat on days when they exercised on an empty stomach than they did on days when they had a small breakfast first. But the difference was negligible and other studies have shown that fewer calories are burned in the long run. Why? The workouts are shorter.

It seems that you can't go very far when your tank is empty. Another study, in the journal *Medicine and Science in Sports and Exercise,* had a group of people ride an exercise bike on two mornings: one day after a small breakfast and the other after eating nothing. The researchers found that when the subjects ate nothing, they became fatigued faster and stopped exercising about thirty minutes earlier. Since most workouts rarely last longer than forty-five minutes, that half an hour can make a huge difference.

One expert that I spoke to, Dr David Prince, an assistant professor at the Albert Einstein College of Medicine in New York, said that when you exercise on an empty tank, your body burns through stored carbohydrates first, then protein, before it finally moves on to fat. In the meantime, he said, 'You lower your blood sugar, causing ravenous hunger that in most people would lead them to eat much more than they would otherwise.'

His recommendation? Try compromising: grab a small piece of fruit, like an apple, which should be just enough to give you energy for a more intense workout.

Do you put on more weight when you eat late at night?

Most of us know strict dieters who stay as far away from food as they can in the hours before bedtime, thinking that any calories they consume in the evening are somehow bound to count more. They usually cite the 'fact' that a person's metabolism slows down significantly in the evening, or that no one burns calories in the middle of the night (except sleepwalkers, of course).

But in reality, a calorie at noon is really no different from a calorie at midnight.

The reason this myth is so widespread may have something to do with skewed perceptions. Many people who eat at night do so after skimping all day, leaving them with a ravenous nocturnal appetite. When they finally get around to eating, they are prone to grabbing the first thing in sight, which – surprise, surprise – is likely to be something quick and easy such as crisps or fast food.

There are also those who eat full meals during the day and decide to eat again at night anyway, packing in extra calories.

People who shed pounds or maintain their weight are less likely to eat as much at night, usually because they get all the calories they need during the day. So by late evening, they have either no cravings at all or they simply manage to control them. In either case, what matters is that they are staying within their caloric limits.

Few studies have actually tested this in humans, largely because doing so would be incredibly labour intensive. It would require closely following people who agreed to change their eating habits drastically while sticking to carefully monitored dietary and exercise habits for weeks, not to mention scrutinizing every single calorie they consumed. (Unfortunately, self-recorded food and exercise diaries aren't always accurate, especially when it comes to guilt-laden snacking, and calorie counting home-cooked meals, as many dieters know, can be a gargantuan task.)

But several studies on animals, including one at the Oregon Health & Science University, USA, in 2003, have examined the claim and shown that night-time calories are no more fattening than daytime ones. The Oregon researchers monitored groups of monkeys that were fed precise amounts of food at various times of the day. Those that ate mostly at night did not put on weight so long as the number of calories they were taking in each day didn't dwarf the number of calories they were burning. As Arlene Spark, an associate professor of nutrition at Hunter College in New York, puts it, 'At the end of the day, the calories you take in must equal the calories you expend.'

One curious side note: a small percentage of people – about 2 per cent of the population – actually have a diagnosable condition that causes them to eat voraciously at night, wake up with no appetite and experience frequent bouts of insomnia. People with this condition, night-eating syndrome, get the vast majority of their calories in the evening, sometimes even rousing themselves from sleep several times a night to gorge on junk food (their most popular food of choice, according to research, is peanut butter).

Interestingly, only a little more than 50 per cent of people with the condition are actually obese (the rest are thin or slightly overweight). There's no cure for the condition, but antidepressants can ease symptoms.

Is yo-yo dieting unhealthy or does it slow down your metabolism?

When it comes to yo-yo dieting, there is only one thing that scientists can agree on: it's extremely common.

Surveys have found that hundreds of thousands, if not millions, of people have experienced it at some point in their lives. Most yo-yo dieters are women, but many men have also adopted yo-yo dieting as a preferred method of weight loss.

But the debate over whether it slows metabolism or ruins your health has – fittingly – been going back and forth for years. Medical experts who warn against it say that the stress of rapidly losing and regaining weight can take a dreadful toll on your body. Others argue that it's better to lose weight any way you can, whenever you can, since there are just too many hazards of remaining overweight, including heart disease, diabetes and breathing problems.

But the truth is not exactly clear cut.

The idea that yo-yoing should be avoided first started gaining ground in 1986, when a study found that rats that had been deprived of food would quickly regain the weight they had lost when they were allowed to eat again, even with fewer calories. The rats, after repeated bouts of starvation, were burning calories less efficiently, and it seemed as though the same effect would be seen in chronic dieters.

But years of research and at least a half a dozen studies have proved that that rush to judgement was wrong. One study, published in the *American Journal of Clinical Nutrition* in 1992, looked at fifty overweight women who dieted frequently, and could not find a shred of evidence that the women had either lower metabolic rates or smaller weight losses over time. But as Cathy Nonas, an obesity expert at North General Hospital in New York City, explained with exasperation, the slow metabolism claim is never going to die. 'We've debunked it many times,' she said. 'But it keeps cropping up.'

But whether yo-yoing can damage your health is another story. While shedding weight is better than remaining overweight, there is evidence that losing weight too rapidly can cause long-term problems. In a study in the *Journal of the American Dietetic Association*, a team of researchers looked at 114 overweight women, two-thirds of them women who had lost more than ten pounds by dieting in the previous twelve years. Those who had yo-yo dieted the most, it turned out, had the lowest levels of natural killer cells – the immune cells that attack viruses and help fight cancer – and even those who had yo-yo dieted only twice showed a decrease. There is also evidence that it lowers your levels of good cholesterol (HDL) and may increase high blood pressure. Why that is isn't really known.

But if you plan on losing weight, there's no question it's better to do it slowly and permanently, with increased exercise and reduced calories. But your metabolism will stay the same, regardless.

Can drinking green tea help you to lose weight?

Way back in 1196, the Japanese Zen priest Eisai wrote the *Kissa Yojoki*, or *Book of Tea*, explaining the wide-ranging health benefits he was certain could be found in green tea – everything from easing indigestion to curing blotchiness to enhancing brain function.

Nearly a thousand years later, people are still trying to prove that a cup of green tea has medicinal powers. And in a culture of fad diets and liposuction, nothing about green tea has sparked as much interest – and as many over-the-counter products – as the claim that it is a potent fat-fighter.

But when it comes to the facts and many other health attributes linked to green tea, you can't count on it. There isn't any solid research demonstrating that loading up on green tea can help you shed pounds.

At the core of the claim is the fact that a typical cup of green tea is packed with catechins, a type of compound with antioxidant properties that supposedly speeds metabolism. Catechins are also thought to increase thermogenesis, the process by which your body burns off fuels like fat. But if there is any difference, it may be too small to notice. One small study showed that drinking green tea regularly could elevate energy expenditure in a twenty-four-hour period by 4 per cent, a level that's considered too small to produce any measurable weight loss. Another study, conducted in the Netherlands, had even less impressive results. Researchers found that people who dieted and then took green tea to stay fit had as much success as those given a placebo.

But the news is not all bad. If you're willing to overload on green tea, you might see some weight-loss benefits. A 2006 study found that in two groups of men who dieted for three months and regularly drank tea, those who drank green tea instead of oolong tea lost, on average, an extra two pounds. The only hitch: the men were given a special green-tea extract each day that contained 690 milligrams of catechins. That's about twenty times the amount found in a typical cup of green tea.

In other words, consuming green-tea extract and following a steady diet may help you lose weight. But don't expect a cup or two of tea each day to make any difference.

Does celery really have negative calories?

Only in an age when people spend hundreds of millions of pounds a year on weight-loss fads, and when eating disorders sometimes seem to be considered fashionable, would anyone dream up a concept like negative calories.

For years, diets and weight-loss books have boasted that there are some foods that burn rather than add calories when you eat them. The idea is that the foods have so few calories that the act of chewing them requires expending more energy than you absorb, resulting in a calorie deficit and, ultimately, weight loss.

Fat chance. It's a concept that has some truth to it, but when you take a closer look, it's not all it's cracked up to be.

At the top of the list of so-called negative-calorie foods are vegetables like cabbage, lettuce, cucumbers and, the most famous, celery. Celery contains eight to ten calories a stalk and is 95 per cent water. Chewing most foods typically burns about five calories an hour. The act of digesting may require slightly more – particularly in the case of celery, since it is mostly cellulose, a type of fibre that humans do not have the necessary enzymes to properly break down and use.

So, mathematically, it is possible that snacking on celery all day could cause a very slight calorie deficit. But the difference would be so minuscule that at the end of the day it wouldn't have any real impact unless the celery was replacing other fattening and high-calorie foods. The other problem is that celery is not only low in calories, it's also low in vitamins and minerals.

If you substitute celery for chocolate and crisps, and those were the things that were pushing the numbers up every time you weighed yourself, then you'd probably lose weight. But realistically speaking, you're not going to lose weight by chewing celery a couple of times a day if you're exercising and eating sensibly.

Over the years, readers have written to me to pitch some clever 'rules' for negative-calorie counting.

John Doherty put forward his mother's insightful theory: 'As she watched the family working feverishly with a variety of implements to extract morsels of crabmeat from the shells, she put forth the hypothesis that we were using more energy removing crabmeat than the crabmeat actually contained. Thus, any theory of negative calories should also factor in the calories used obtaining the food in the first place.'

Leonard J. Kelly suggested a rule that works in favour of beer drinkers: 'It has been held that if you drink your beer very cold, it has, in fact, negative calories. Those who hold to that theory say that the energy needed to bring the beer to body temperature is in fact greater than the calorie content of the beer itself.' Lisa G. Westheimer proposed, 'When overeating calorie-rich foods, do so in multiples. Your body can count only so high. Thus, anything eaten above the amount your body can count up to has no calories . . . With pancakes, the body can only recognize the first six. Anything after that is gravy (or syrup, if you want to be technical).'

And Stephen H. Kaufman concocted a scheme that's hard to resist: 'The food you don't eat – at a party, reception, cocktail gathering, etc. – is subtracted from your total intake. For example, someone brings rich chocolate cake to the office for a colleague's birthday. You pass. Those 400 or so calories, plus all that cholesterol and fat, are put on a credit line in your fat account. Whatever else you eat that day, you start with minus 400 calories.'

They all seem to have as much scientific credence as negative-calorie celery.

4
Eat, Drink, Be Merry?

In a pickle over what (not) to eat

When it comes to food, most of us are forced to perform a balancing act. We are yanked in one direction by our desire to look and feel good and pulled in the other by our desire to eat what looks and tastes good. And beyond our obsession with food and its ability to ignite our taste buds and soothe our palate, there is also a fascination with its ability to heal, sicken and hypnotize us.

No wonder there are so many old wives' tales and bromides that revolve around food, factoring into (nearly) every mealtime decision, which means nearly all the time on any given day. Take my typical day:

8:30 a.m. Rise and shine. I wake up, roll out of bed, brush my teeth, take a quick shower. Make sure my boss hasn't called about a crisis at the newspaper. OK, it's time to get some food. After all, breakfast is the most important meal of the day, right – or is it? Maybe my mum was wrong, and that message on the cereal box, too.

9 a.m. No time for breakfast anyway – one foot is out the door. But I definitely need a quick boost. I know, tea. The green kind. They say it's the best one: cures cancer, keeps you healthy. Or so I've read.

9:30 a.m. At my desk, ready to go to sleep. This tea is not working. Skipping breakfast was not a good idea. Must be why my energy levels are through the floor. It's time to upgrade to coffee. And a cereal bar.

1 p.m. Lunch. I am *starving*. The cafeteria is serving tuna. Perfect: fish is brain food. At least that's what they say. Better get a salad, too – carrots are good for the eyes. And God knows my eyesight is shot. Nearly walked into a door a few minutes ago.

3 p.m. Yawn. Post-lunch stupor. I need a jolt: more caffeine. This article I'm working on is not, I repeat, not going to write itself. A soft drink sounds good. Better make it a diet – no sugar, no calories, plenty of caffeine. *Perfect!* But then again, diet soft drinks have all that artificial sweetener in them. I've heard that stuff will kill you.

Hmm . . .

3:03 p.m. Thought about it for a couple of minutes. Decide to drink the soft drink anyway.

6 p.m. Early dinner. Better make it a quick one. Promised a couple of friends we'd grab some drinks after work. And I can't drink on an empty stomach – not with these guys. Need something heavy, but something fast. Chicken. That new joint down the street has amazing grilled fajitas. But what was that I read about grilled meat causing cancer the other day?

7:30 p.m. I make it to the bar, thirty minutes late. Garren gives me grief. But Dave doesn't seem to mind. Well, you can't please everybody.

7:35 p.m. The waiter comes by: decision time. Is this a beer night or wine night? Can't drink both: mixing makes you sick. Better start with beer, then finish off with wine. After all, beer then wine, fine; wine then beer, oh dear. Garren disagrees, believing that it's the other way around. Dave disagrees with us both: it doesn't make a difference, he says.

We are all confused.

9 p.m. My stomach is killing me. Must have been the tuna. I can only blame myself because I broke my rule never to trust the cafeteria food. Better drink up: doesn't alcohol cure food poisoning? Thank you, alcohol, for killing salmonella, E. coli, and all those other nasty bugs.

I know I read about this in a study somewhere. It was in that journal, called . . . umm . . . Ugh, no idea. Feels like I can't remember a thing right now – must be all those lost brain cells. Thank you, alcohol, for that as well.

11 p.m. I stumble into bed. No way I'm taking a shower right now. Mental note: brush teeth twice tomorrow morning and stay away from tuna!

Is breakfast really the most important meal of the day?

In a workaholic culture where people are never really off the clock – constantly tethered to their BlackBerries, their mobile phones and their laptops – maybe it's no surprise that even breakfast has become too time-consuming a chore to endure. Most people seem content just to grab a cup of coffee as they bolt out the door, ignoring that faint, motherly voice in their heads urging them to sit down for a real meal.

The 'breakfast-is-the-most-important-meal' claim may sound like more of a marketing ploy from cereal advertisements than a scientific fact. But it turns out that mothers everywhere were right.

People who eat a normal breakfast each morning – usually consisting of fibre and a protein source like eggs, meat or soy – have been shown in repeated studies to be healthier than those who do not. The most immediate benefits from breakfast are increased energy levels and a better ability to concentrate during the day (especially true with school-aged children, scientists say). But it is also clear that eating breakfast can help ward off disease.

In a study at Harvard Medical School, researchers tracked thousands of people and found that those who ate breakfast every day were far less likely to be obese than those who skipped it. Again, part of the reason is that people who skimp on meals in the morning – whether for lack of time or in the hope of losing weight – tend to compensate by gorging later in the day, often on junk food. No surprise, then, that people who regularly skip breakfast and end up with less than ideal diets are also twice as likely to develop insulin resistance syndrome, a metabolic disorder that can lead to diabetes and coronary heart disease.

For many people, breakfast is also the greatest source in their diet of wholegrain foods, which are associated with better health and a longer lifespan. Wholegrains are the main ingredients in some breads and cereals and they're rich in antioxidants, minerals and fibre. A study following 34,000 women for more than a decade found that those who ate at least one serving of wholegrain foods each day – usually during breakfast – reduced their rate of death from all causes during the study period by about 25 per cent.

Turns out those fifteen minutes you save by skipping breakfast each day might cost you later on.

Is eating fish good for the brain?

When it comes to yet another piece of dietary advice that many of us were brought up on, the old wisdom prevails: fish is food for the brain. One evolutionary theory even suggests that humans evolved in coastal areas because certain nutrients in fish, omega-3 fatty acids in particular, were necessary for brain development.

For years, fish was one of the primary sources of animal protein in people's diets. But lately it has begun to slip far behind red meat and poultry, an unfortunate decline fuelled largely by concerns about PCB and mercury contamination. The average person today eats about three fewer pounds of fish every year than they did twenty years ago. While it's right to be concerned about contaminants, studies suggest that you can still get the brainy benefits of fish without the risk by eating it only twice a week and choosing the type carefully.

By far the best benefits of fish can be found in its fat. For fish to survive in cold water, their fats have to be in liquid form, and liquid fats are polyunsaturated. But unlike the polyunsaturated oils found in foods like corn and soybeans, fish oil contains high amounts of two omega-3 fatty acids – EPA and DHA – that benefit the heart and blood vessels and are essential to normal brain development. These fatty acids have been shown to lower blood pressure, block substances that cause inflammation, reduce the formation of blood clots and prevent cardiovascular damage caused by triglycerides. That's a fat anyone could love.

Some of the benefits of eating fish may also stem from the fact that it takes the place of red meat in the diet. Either way, there is overwhelming evidence that a diet rich in fish can keep the mind sharp, protecting it against Alzheimer's disease and other ills of ageing. One study in the *Archives of Neurology* found that elderly people who ate fish at least once a week did better on tests of memory and mental acuity than their peers who did not. They also had a 10 per cent slower decline in mental skills each year and those who ate twice as much fish showed a 13 per cent slower annual decline during the course of the six-year study.

In fact, fish is good for the brain at all stages of life. Another study looked at 135 mothers and their infants, finding that the more fish the mothers ate during their second trimesters, the better their infants did on cognitive tests when they were six months old.

Yet, because pregnant women and breastfeeding mothers are most vulnerable to the effects of contaminants found in fish, it's best that women in these groups stick to canned light tuna or salmon and steer clear of fish with high mercury levels. This goes for other adults as well. The fish most likely to be contaminated are large deep-sea species that are closer to the top of the food chain, such as shark, swordfish, king mackerel and tilefish.

For people who don't enjoy eating fish or would rather get the benefits without any risk at all, there are plenty of supplements that can do the job. Most omega-3 supplements are about the same in quality and purity, so it's best to pick them based on price. A cheap one is usually just as good as the most expensive.

But for those who prefer to stick to the real thing, there are plenty of varieties of fish, from anchovies to tilapia, that are high in nutrients and low in contaminants. The best options and the worst offenders, based on research on those two criteria carried out by Environmental Defense, a leading advocacy group, are as follows:

The Best:

Abalone (US farmed)
Anchovies
Arctic Char
Catfish
Clams
Crab (Dungeness, snow, stone)
Crawfish (US)
Pacific halibut (Alaskan)
Herring
Mahimahi (US Atlantic)
Mussels (farmed)
Oysters (farmed)
Sablefish/black cod (Alaskan)
Salmon (wild, pink/sockeye)
Sardines
Scallops (farmed)
Shrimp
Spot prawns
Striped bass (farmed)
Sturgeon
Tilapia

The Worst:

Bluefin tuna
Caviar (wild)
Chilean sea bass/toothfish
Atlantic cod
Grouper
Atlantic halibut
Marlin
Monkfish/goosefish

Orange roughy
Rockfish/rock cod (Pacific)
Atlantic salmon (farmed)
Shark
Imported shrimp and prawns

Skate
Snapper
Wild sturgeon
Imported swordfish
Tilefish

Does eating carrots improve your eyesight?

Most children have probably never heard the name John 'Cat's Eyes' Cunningham before. But many have no doubt suffered hours of frustration at the dinner table because of something he did more than sixty years ago.

In 1940, Cunningham, a slight, amiable captain in the Royal Air Force, became the first pilot to shoot down an enemy aircraft – and subsequently many more – using a newfangled invention called radar.

At the time, the military was desperate to keep its secret new invention under wraps, so government officials attributed Cunningham's uncanny ability to spot enemy aircraft at night to his odd love of carrots. Sounds ridiculous. But pretty soon, newspapers were claiming that the sudden increase in downed German fighter planes was a direct result of the fact that all RAF pilots were being fed obscene amounts of carrots, which vastly improved their night vision.

The radar secret was eventually let out of the bag. But the claim that carrots can improve your eyesight stuck, and perhaps for good reason.

Carrots are high in beta-carotene, a component of vitamin A, which is critical to normal vision. It's no coincidence that in countries where rice is a dietary staple, but carrots and other sources of the vitamin are scarce, poor vision is rampant.

So should you forget about glasses and just eat carrots? Probably not. Studies show that while taking vitamin A can reverse poor vision caused by a deficiency, it will not strengthen your eyesight or slow the decline of vision in people who are healthy.

A study by researchers at The Johns Hopkins University, Baltimore, Maryland, in 1998, for example, looked at thirty thousand women in South Asia at high risk of vitamin deficiencies. It found that a group that received vitamin A tablets had 67 per cent fewer cases of night blindness than a group that received a placebo. But in 2003, researchers at Brigham And Women's Hospital in Boston, USA, found that thousands of healthy men who took beta-carotene pills for twelve years had the same rate of age-related cataracts as those given a placebo. The only benefit was seen in smokers, a group whose habit puts them at greater risk of developing cataracts to begin with. The smokers in that study who took beta-carotene lowered their cataract risk by an astounding 25 per cent.

Cunningham, meanwhile, a decorated World War II veteran, died a hero in 2002. But the old wives' tale which he inspired lives on at dinner tables everywhere.

Are beets good for your liver?

They are known among health nuts throughout the world as potent detoxifiers that cleanse the blood. But beets may have gained their strongest reputation because they are so abundant in the Caucasus area of Russia, a region densely populated with centenarians, despite the popularity of vodka. Some experts think the diet, which is heavy in pickled beets and borscht, or beet soup, may explain why some of the people there live so long.

Studies on animals have indeed found that a pigment in red beets called betalain can slightly elevate levels of an enzyme that helps fight cancer in liver cells, and that the pigment might also help to protect against other diseases, like colon cancer. The enzymes are specifically thought to detoxify carcinogens and purge them from the body.

There's just one small problem. Ever notice how beets can give your urine a reddish tinge? That's because many people don't have the ability to digest red-beet pigment; it just passes right through their digestive systems – with presumably little or no effect on the liver.

Beets, it should be mentioned, are also packed with disease-fighting antioxidants such as beta-carotene, carotenoids and flavonoids. But then again, so are most fruits and vegetables.

Beets may be good for the liver, but really not any more so than a lot of other yummy things you can find in your local produce aisle.

Can having a glass of wine with your meal prevent food poisoning?

By now, everyone knows that a little alcohol from time to time can prevent heart disease and help ward off dementia. But a lesser known claim is that alcohol can have more immediate health benefits, acting as an antiseptic of sorts that can protect you against bacterial evils.

Sounds like just another old wives' tale. But go ahead, have a drink with your meal. This one is actually true.

To get to the facts, scientists have studied outbreaks of food poisoning at large social gatherings, carefully teasing apart which guests got sick, which ones didn't, and why. In 2002, for example, health officials in Spain studied a salmonella outbreak that struck people who had the bad fortune of being served bad tuna and potato salad at a large banquet in Castellon. More than fifty people at the banquet were exposed to salmonella through the food, but not all of them got sick.

Although nearly all of the people who were exposed to the salmonella and drank only non-alcoholic beverages at the banquet became acutely ill, only 78 per cent of those who ate the contaminated food but also had one or two drinks got sick. In addition, only half of those who were exposed but had three or more drinks became ill. Other Spanish studies, too, have found that people who drank the largest amounts of alcohol at social events traced to large salmonella outbreaks emerged with the lowest levels of sickness.

Alcohol, it seems, has true medicinal powers. Who knew that old troublemaker Jose Cuervo could actually serve a useful purpose after college?

But if you plan on having a glass of liquor with your suspect dinner, definitely make it a double. There is good evidence that a drink may need to be stiff for alcohol's protective effect to kick in. Studies of large, oyster-borne outbreaks of hepatitis A have shown that only drinks with an alcohol concentration of at least 10 per cent have any protective effect. In other words, if you're a beer drinker and you're having tuna salad at a wedding, consider treating yourself to a glass of wine or two at some point during your meal.

The effect may have something to do with alcohol's ability to strongly stimulate gastric acid secretions in the stomach, which creates a lethal environment for germs and bacteria. Wine, surprisingly, is particularly potent when it comes to this because grapes also have well-known antibacterial properties. Chardonnay and other white wines seem to work the best, probably because they are slightly more acidic than reds. But either colour is likely to do the trick. You'll certainly be better off than the poor sap in the corner sipping a soft drink.

Does alcohol really kill brain cells?

When the ancient Greeks wanted to reassure a guest at a dinner party that their wine had not been spiked with poison, they toasted to good health.

Although wine laced with poison is certainly less of a worry today than it was back then, there remain other hazards from indulging in a love of drink – raging hangovers, of course, being the most common.

But one thing people who drink socially don't need to worry about is sacrificing their brain cells: people who drink regularly and at times even heavily are not in danger of losing neurons.

The notion that alcohol wipes out brain cells has been around for decades. Many studies have linked heavy drinking with mental deficits, and long-term damage from years of heavy drinking has been well documented. The developing brain is particularly vulnerable to alcohol's effects, putting teenagers and foetuses at greatest risk.

Because alcohol is a powerful disinfectant, in high concentrations it can damage or kill off human cells. But the blood alcohol concentrations that make a person buzzed or drunk – 0.1 per cent or greater – are far below the extremely high concentrations that are lethal to cells (sterilizers, for example, are typically 100 per cent alcohol solutions). Even a person who drank non-stop would almost certainly stop breathing (alcohol causes respiratory depression) and hit the floor long before their blood alcohol level got anywhere near 1 per cent.

73

This has been confirmed through more direct approaches. In one study, the brains of heavy drinkers who died of non-alcohol-related causes were compared with those of non-alcoholics of similar age and background: both groups showed roughly the same number and density of neurons.

But while it may not kill brain cells per se, heavy alcohol use can cause long-term damage. Most of the damage is caused by the disruption of message-carrying dendrites attached to neurons in the cerebellum, a brain structure that's involved in learning and motor coordination. In the short term, it causes the hallmarks of intoxication that we're all familiar with: slow reflexes, loss of inhibition and slurred speech. In the long term, it permanently reduces communication between neurons and alters their structure.

And there is another caveat. While alcohol itself does not directly kill off brain cells, heavy drinking can lead to cell death in other ways. Alcoholics tend to ignore their health and diets, which puts them at high risk of developing Wernicke-Korsakoff syndrome, a severe disorder that ravages the memory and stems from a thiamine deficiency.

One 1999 study compared the brains of alcoholics with Wernicke-Korsakoff to the brains of other alcoholics and non-drinkers. While the Wernicke-Korsakoff brains all showed a drastic reduction in cell density in the cerebellum, there was little difference between alcoholics who did not develop the syndrome and normal subjects, suggesting that it was largely a lack of thiamine in the Wernicke-Korsakoff patients that killed off their cells (not the alcohol per se).

Definitely a buzz kill.

Do women get drunk faster than men?

Even a woman who drank with Hemingway and has a martini named in her honour, Dorothy Parker, the heavy-drinking, acid-tongued writer and poet, acknowledged that she could rarely handle more than two martinis at most – 'Three I'm under the table, four I'm under the host,' she once said.

Simple observation suggests that Parker is not alone: women in general feel the effects of alcohol more quickly than men. But while most people chalk it up to average differences in size, the scientific explanation is that it has more to do with body composition.

Because women's bodies have a higher ratio of fat to water, they reach a higher blood alcohol concentration after a single drink than men, even when matched for weight and size. Enzymes also play a role. A landmark study published in the

New England Journal of Medicine in 1990 found that in women, levels of gastric alcohol dehydrogenase, a compound that breaks down alcohol, are on average nearly half what they are in men. It also found that the amount of alcohol metabolized after its first passage through a woman's liver and stomach is about 20 per cent what it is in men.

Women just aren't very efficient at digesting alcohol, regardless of their size. Compared to men, a greater percentage of alcohol hits the bloodstream and goes straight to the brain. No one knows why that is. But as a result, women who drink heavily develop cirrhosis and other alcohol-induced diseases sooner than male drinkers.

The silver lining? Women who indulge in a drink or two a day have lower rates of heart attacks, cardiovascular problems and Alzheimer's disease than those who prefer their drinks alcohol-free. Like blondes, they also have more fun.

Is it all that bad to drink on an empty stomach?

It's an age-old rule about drinking, one that everyone knows and most people have broken: always fill up on food before filling up on alcohol.

Common wisdom, of course, suggests a straightforward reason, that drinking on an empty stomach will lead to intoxication more quickly. But just how much of a difference does eating before imbibing really make?

According to several studies and experts on alcohol, a lot. Mostly it has to do with the way liquor is metabolized in the stomach and small intestine. Whenever a person consumes alcohol, the body starts to break it down immediately, but some is always absorbed directly into the bloodstream.

Having food in the stomach – particularly proteins, fats and dense carbohydrates – slows down that absorption process.

Things that speed it up are carbonated mixers, like soda (the gas in fizzy drinks increases the rate of absorption, which is why champagne acts so quickly), and higher temperatures. Warm drinks are absorbed faster than cold ones.

One study in 1994 demonstrated the empty-stomach claim by having a group of ten people consume a few drinks on two separate days. In one case they drank after an overnight fast, and in the other, they drank after they ate a modest breakfast. On the day the subjects ate, the rate of intoxication was slower, even though the amount of alcohol had not changed. But the subjects also reached significantly lower blood-alcohol levels overall – on average about 70 per cent of what they were on the day they skipped breakfast.

In some cases, having a meal before drinking kept a person from climbing above a blood alcohol level of 0.08 per cent – the legal blood-alcohol limit for driving in the UK. For a man who weighs 170 pounds, reaching that level on an empty stomach takes only four twelve-ounce cans of beer. For a woman who weighs 137 pounds, it takes less than three. Although every metabolism works differently, for the average person it takes at least seven long hours to return to a completely sober state from a drunken one.

Once that alcohol is in your system, none of the things people say will get it out faster – coffee, a cold shower – will actually accomplish that. All you can do is drink lots of water and make plenty of trips to the bathroom.

What about mixing different types of alcohol – does it make you sick?

Too much alcohol of any kind is rarely a good idea, but there are those people who claim that mixing beer and liquor, particularly in that order, can also be a hazard.

Some even know it by rhyme. 'Beer before liquor, never been sicker,' goes one old saying, while older drinkers tend to remember it as, 'Beer on whisky, awful risky; whisky on beer, never fear.'

There are probably a hundred ways to say it, and even more theories on how it got started. One possibility is that it has something to do with the way certain alcoholic beverages are digested. Carbonated drinks like beer, champagne and sparkling wines, for example, are absorbed into the blood-stream more quickly because they tend to irritate the lining of the stomach. Starting with beer and then adding wine or liquor, as a result, can theoretically lead to intoxication more quickly.

But in reality, that would have only a small, and barely noticeable, effect. What matters most is the amount of alcohol a person is consuming and whether it's combined with any food, which slows absorption and minimizes sickness.

But there's another explanation for the popular 'beer before liquor' claim, argued Carlton K. Erickson, the director of the Addiction Science Research and Education Centre at the University of Texas College of Pharmacy. Mostly, it has to do with the order in which people typically consume their drinks.

'Most people do not drink a lot of beer after they've had liquor,' Erickson pointed out.

'The pattern, more often, is that people will have beer and then move on to liquor at the end of the night, and so they think it's the liquor that made them sick,' he continued. 'But simply mixing the two really has nothing to do with it.'

Maybe it's time to update the saying: 'Lots to drink, sure to be sick.'

Well, poetry was never my strong point.

Will eating poppy seeds make you fail a drug test?

This fear stems from the well-known fact that some of the most addictive drugs known to man – heroin, opium and morphine – and one of the most pleasant and widely used cooking ingredients – the poppy seed – all derive from the same source, the opium poppy. That a drugs test could confuse poppy seeds with a powerful drug has the ring of urban legend, but it is absolutely true.

All it takes is eating two or three slices of bread or bagels heavily coated with poppy seeds to end up with abnormal levels of morphine circulating in your system for hours, which could lead some routine drugs tests to come back positive, and many toxicologists can cite specific instances of that happening. A subsequent test can rule out heroin, though not other opiates, by looking for a specific metabolite, 6-acetylmorphine, though someone who has a poppy-seed bagel for breakfast and is tested later that day would still have far lower levels of morphine than a person who, for example, abuses painkillers.

But for that reason, the US federal government recently raised the threshold for opiates in workplace testing, from three hundred nanograms a millilitre to two thousand. With the new limit, you'd have to consume something in the range of about a dozen bagels to fail the test.

One expert, Dr Timothy P. Rohrig of the Regional Forensic Science Centre in Kansas, USA, said the new test is designed to be reasonable. If someone tested well above the two thousand nanogram per millilitre limit and 'tried to explain it by saying they ate fifteen bagels for lunch, it would sound absurd,' he said. On the other hand, if a person failed the test and claimed to be using cough syrup with an opiate like codeine to fight off a cold, they might sound more believable, and could even win a second chance (hint, hint).

All of this raises another important question: if it's possible to test positive for opium after eating a couple of poppy-seed bagels, does that mean you can get stoned too?

Well, don't count on it. Since you're eating the poppies and not smoking them, you'll end up feeling full long before you feel anything else.

Are spots triggered by what you eat?

Despite what parents everywhere have long insisted, most of us know by now that chocolate and greasy foods won't cause acne. The average person stops believing that particular lie after primary school. But it would be foolish to assume that what we put in our bodies has absolutely no effect on our skin – so what about other foods?

What scientists know for certain is that acne is largely influenced by genetics and hormonal fluctuations, hence the tendency for it to develop during puberty, pregnancy and menopause, when our hormones are out of whack. Which brings me to my next point: no one associates milk and cheese with bad skin, but besides fat and salt, these two foods, like all dairy products, are also high in something else: hormones.

All those parents who have scared their kids with tales of chocolate and French fries fuelling hideous breakouts apparently never stopped to think about this. But scientists have (perhaps a few inspired by their own teenage anxiety and acne).

Back in 2005, scientists at Harvard University (please see previous parenthetical statement) discovered the dairy trigger after analyzing the habits and diets of nearly fifty thousand people, looking especially at what they ate in high school. People who drank three or more cups of milk a day, it turned out, were 22 per cent more likely to experience severe acne than their classmates who drank one serving a week or less. Skimmed milk, for some reason, had the greatest effect. Cream cheese and cottage cheese were also associated with outbreaks, while chocolate and greasy foods were not.

Foods that contain iodides, like shellfish and soy sauce, also seem to exacerbate acne, and for good reason. Iodides are thought to play a role in inflammation.

Another acne claim that bursts under scrutiny? That it flares up in the summer and gets better in the winter. Generally, seasonal impact varies from person to person. But a study in the *Journal of Dermatology* in 2002 looked at 452 people with acne and found that 56 per cent said they had worse symptoms in the summer, while only 11 per cent experienced more outbreaks in the winter.

It makes sense that symptoms would wane in the summer, even with the regular appearance of the ice-cream truck. Greater exposure to light, particularly ultraviolet light, destroys acne-causing bacteria. One large study found that treatment with light works better than benzoyl peroxide, a standard over-the-counter treatment and a common ingredient in products aimed at preventing spots.

But don't run out and crisp yourself in the sun with a solar reflector propped on your chest just yet. Instead of exposing yourself to cancer-causing wavelengths for hours on end, you can go to a dermatologist's office and sit under a machine that delivers light without the harmful wavelengths. Plus it beats fighting traffic on the way to the beach.

Does grilled meat cause cancer?

Nothing signals the arrival of summer quite so much as the barbecue coming out in the back garden. But the news these last few years has been terrible for barbecue fans everywhere. Firstly, global warming made the prospect of standing outside in front of an open flame all day sound as appealing as spending a night locked in a tanning booth. Then, in the spring of 2005, just in time for barbecue season, the US Department of Health and Human Services quietly added heterocyclic amines – a type of compound that forms in red meat, poultry and fish on the grill – to its list of carcinogens. That bit of news made a grim situation worse. At least one other group of chemicals, polycyclic aromatic hydrocarbons, which also collect on meat cooked over hot coals, has been on the agency's list since 1981.

Sitting around a barbecue with friends is one of my favourite summer activities, so I took off my apron and donned my reporter's cap to find out more. It goes without saying that all of us at some point or another have eaten a piece of food and pretended that an ingredient or two it contained wasn't there. If we didn't lie to ourselves like this on occasion, we would all go hungry.

But grilled meat is different. Neither of the two suspect chemicals mentioned earlier are pleasant. Heterocyclic amines are created when creatinine, an amino acid found in meat, is broken down at high temperatures. They can form on your steak or fillet whether you're grilling it, broiling it or searing it in a frying pan. Using a countertop grill to cook your meat is no different. Polycyclic aromatic hydrocarbons, meanwhile, are chemicals that contaminate meat through smoke that's created by fat dripping on hot coals or charcoal briquettes. The chemicals get in your food when the smoke drifts back upward.

Hungry yet?

The good news when it comes to polycyclic aromatic hydrocarbons is that because they're created in part by hot coals, you can avoid them simply by using a gas grill.

Concerns about the two types of chemicals stem largely from epidemiological studies. In 1999, for example, researchers at the National Cancer Institute conducted a large study of colorectal cancer and found that the odds of developing the disease were tightly linked to consumption of red meat, particularly when grilled or well done. Another study in 2002 looked at more than eight hundred people and found that those who ate the most grilled or barbecued meat seemed to double their risk of developing pancreatic cancer, even after the researchers adjusted for smoking, age and other risk factors.

But the news is not all grim – far from it. You don't have to ditch the apron and abandon the time-honoured art of the barbecue just yet. Here are some tips that can lower your risk:

- Since these two carcinogens are found in meat cooked at high temperatures or exposed to flare-ups, you should preheat your food in a microwave, which reduces the time it needs to spend on the grill.

- Marinating has been shown to have a strong protective effect, probably because the liquid prevents burning. According to some sources, even marinating for a few minutes can reduce the amount of heterocyclic amines formed by as much as 99 per cent. It's best to use marinades that are spicy or contain an acidic base, like citrus juice or vinegar, and to limit the amount of oil you use to prevent flare-ups. You should use about a half-cup of marinade for every pound of meat. You don't have to completely immerse or drown the food, but it should be turned occasionally. Fish needs about twenty minutes in marinade and poultry and red meat require about forty-five minutes.

- Go for meats that are lean and well-trimmed, since they have less fat that can drip into the flames. Chicken cutlets, shrimp, fish and lean pieces of meat are probably your best bets, while ribs and sausages – both extremely high in fat – are not. You should also keep your cuts of meat small, so they have less surface area and don't need as much time on the grill.

- Try to keep a spray bottle filled with water nearby so you can control any flare-ups. And instead of placing your food directly on the grill, cover the grate with punctured aluminium foil. This not only protects your food against smoke and flare-ups, but also keeps fatty juices from dripping into the flames or coals.

- Stay away from charred or blackened foods! These are the parts that are particularly hazardous. Always trim them off and push them to the side before digging in.

- Finally, pile on the veggies. It's the chemicals in grilled meat you need to avoid. Grilled veggies you can eat to your heart's content without a worry.

5
Toxic Planet

It's a dangerous world out there,
PART I

We are healthier, smarter, more advanced, longer lived and we have more luxuries and conveniences than we ever had before. We spend more and more on regulations designed to protect us from the hazards of our industrial and agricultural products, and yet the result of all this is that we also spend an inordinate amount of time obsessing over the invisible toxins that might lurk in the cities, the homes, the drugs, the toys, the treats and the contraptions that we have invented to make our lives squeaky clean.

This, of course, is not to say that the risks and hazards that we worry about are not real. Mass-produced foods do make us fatter and diabetic, drug-resistant bacteria and viruses do expose us to ghastly diseases, and many industrial pollutants do drive up the rates of cancer. We simply cannot avoid every risk. So, on occasion, we are bound to fall victim to the toxic products of our man-made environment.

But is it possible that we worry too much? Is it possible that our anxiety-inducing obsessions with these toxic risks are out of proportion to the actual hazards that they pose?

Many of us buy pricey antibacterial soaps and use them religiously, but how many of us look at the ingredients in our air-fresheners before we spray them around the house? There are people who won't drink water from a tap, but will speed on the motorway, eat at a fast-food chain, roast themselves in a tanning booth or pay someone for the chance to parachute out of a moving plane – all activities that can carry great risks. And how many smokers would complain about pollution if they lived next to a smokestack?

So why do we freak out about tainted spinach and deadly deodorants and not about other things that seem more likely to hurt us? According to psychologists who study risk perception, what it comes down to is control. When the risk is one that is voluntarily assumed and not imposed on us, then we tend to become complacent.

So, what are the risks of the plastics, chemicals and all the other artificial stuff we've added to the world?

Are artificial sweeteners bad for you?

How sweet it is . . . aspartame, that is.

This chemical freak of nature and sugar impersonator, commonly found in packets of sweetener, is a staggering two hundred times as sweet as the plain old sucrose sitting in your kitchen cupboard. Then there is saccharin, which is – get this – two hundred to seven hundred times as sweet as sugar! And yet somehow both of these sweeteners have little or no effect on blood sugar and virtually no calories.

I have always found that amazing. But even more fascinating is that for decades artificial sweeteners have been linked to everything from cancer to seizures to headaches. And none more so than aspartame. Fears about aspartame have haunted the sweetener from the day it was approved, and have been inflamed repeatedly by dubious studies ever since.

The flames have mostly been fanned by reports on the Internet. The best part is that, according to research, one solitary woman is the source of the rumour that aspartame causes almost every illness known to man. This prolific and anonymous woman has argued that most of the studies of aspartame can't be trusted because they were financed by the company that created it, G. D. Searle, which supposedly has withheld evidence of its dangers.

Conspiracy theories aside, there have been a lot of thorough, independent studies of aspartame, and most have cleared it of any hazards. Its proponents like to point out that the components of aspartame – phenylalanine, aspartic acid and a tiny amount of methanol – are found in much larger amounts in dairy products, meats and fruit juices, and that they are metabolized no differently.

One widely promoted claim is that aspartame is responsible for a rise in brain tumours. But studies show that brain tumours were on the rise long before aspartame was introduced and of course plenty of other hazards have been blamed for the rise, such as mobile phones. (More on that later.)

Some research has linked aspartame to lymphoma, including a 2005 Italian study that showed that rats that consumed the equivalent of four to five bottles of diet soft drinks a day had an increase in cancer. But studies carried out by the National Cancer Institute looked at hundreds of thousands of humans and found no elevated risk, even among the heaviest users of aspartame.

That side of the debate rages on. Meanwhile, one of the more mysterious reported side effects is among the most commonly mentioned: headaches. Migraine sufferers are sometimes known to steer clear of aspartame and other sweeteners, if only to be on the safe side. That is probably a good idea. While the evidence is not strong, there is certainly some scientific basis for the link. A study in the journal *Neurology* followed people who complained of headaches brought on by sweeteners and did find that on days they were exposed to sweeteners – instead of a similar-tasting placebo given on other days – they had slightly more headaches.

The science on sweeteners will continue for years, but in the meantime, here are some interesting titbits:

- The most intense natural sugar substitute is a thousand times sweeter than sucrose and is known in its country of origin, Gabon, as *l'oubli*, which is French for 'forgetfulness', because it's so sweet it'll make you forget your own name.

- P-4000 is one of the strongest sweeteners known to man. It is four thousand times as sweet as sucrose.

- At the time aspartame was approved in 1981, its maker, G. D. Searle, was headed by former US Secretary of Defense and accidental poet Donald Rumsfeld.

Can soft drinks cause cancer?

Drinking too many soft drinks has its hazards – obesity and a higher risk of diabetes chief among them. But researchers in India spawned a debate a few years ago when they suggested that the list should include oesophageal cancer, a deadly disease with a low survival rate.

Their assertion was based largely on two observations: the high acidic content of fizzy drinks and a sharp rise in oesophageal cancer that seemed to coincide with the growing popularity of soft drinks. Take the United States, for example. In the last fifty years alone, Americans increased their annual consumption of soft drinks from 11 gallons in 1946 to a staggering 42 gallons in 2000. At the same time, cases of oesophageal cancer have more than tripled.

Then there was this: carbonated drinks not only cause a phenomenon known as gastric distension – which irritates the lower portion of the oesophagus – they have also been linked to heartburn, a known risk factor for oesophageal cancer. Besides, soft drinks have been a favourite target. Like the conspiracy theories about aspartame, rumours that other additives in fizzy drinks, including benzene, are slowly killing us have been circulating on the Internet for years. To some, the link to oesophageal cancer was an open-and-shut case.

But the connection was based largely on circumstantial evidence, which left many scientists sceptical and, it now appears, for good reason: extensive studies have examined the Indian researchers' claims and burst their fizzy bubbles.

One of the largest studies was published in the USA in the *Journal of the National Cancer Institute*. Conducted by a team at Yale, the study looked at the diets and levels of soft-drink consumption among nearly two thousand people, about half of whom had oesophageal cancer, in four different states. But instead of finding that soft drinks somehow contribute to the development of the disease, the study found the opposite. People who drank the most soft drinks were actually less likely to develop oesophageal cancer – and those who drank diet soft drinks had the lowest rate of all, half the risk of developing oesophageal cancer as those who avoided it.

But if you're a calorie counter don't get too excited. It's not likely that diet soft drinks have any special protective effects against cancer. It's just that people who prefer diet beverages are generally more health conscious than their peers. If you're more likely to exercise, eat well, avoid cigarettes and take good care of your body – all things that lower your risk of developing cancer – then, statistically, you're more likely to drink diet soft drinks.

Do antiperspirants really cause Alzheimer's disease?

The scare began about twenty years ago, when scientists noticed that the sick brains of people with Alzheimer's disease had high levels of aluminium, prompting people to throw out their pots and pans, cast a suspicious eye on tinfoil and shun anti-perspirants, antacids, and other household products that contain aluminium, a known neurotoxin. Like a 1950s sci-fi movie plot, the thought was that the aluminium in antiperspirants would seep into your armpits, invade your bloodstream and eventually settle in your brain, turning it into mush.

But in the real world, there's no reason to sweat it. Scientists have thoroughly debunked the idea.

What now seems pretty clear is that those high levels of aluminium found in the brains of Alzheimer's patients were a result, not a cause, of the disease. Weak or dying brain cells lose the ability to eliminate toxins, making them more likely to contain high levels of aluminium, which is so widespread (it's the third most common element on Earth) that everyone is exposed to it.

Because aluminium is present in laboratory dust and in the stains that researchers use to prepare brain tissue for examination, it is also likely that some of the aluminium discovered in the brains of Alzheimer's patients was simply laboratory contaminants. When one group of British researchers tested this hypothesis in the early 1990s by using nuclear microscopy – a method that involves bombarding tissue with protons instead of staining it – they found no signs of aluminium in 105 plaques taken from the brains of Alzheimer's patients.

There have also been rigorous epidemiological studies that threw cold water on the claim. One, published in 2002, followed about 4,600 people for several years and found no increased risk of Alzheimer's in people who regularly used antiperspirants or antacids.

With so much evidence, you may be wondering if aluminium can be absorbed through the armpits at all. The answer is yes – but only in extremely microscopic quantities. In general, a person absorbs no more than four micrograms of aluminium during a single use of antiperspirant on both underarms.

How much is a microgram? If you chopped a thumb tack into a couple of million pieces, one of those pieces would be a microgram. Here's another way to look at it. Four micrograms is about 2.5 per cent of the aluminium your gut would absorb from the food you ate between the time you applied the antiperspirant and when you washed it off. In other words, if you're concerned about aluminium, antiperspirant is one of the last things you should worry about.

If you're like most people, you've probably also noticed that regular deodorant doesn't stop you from sweating – it just masks your body odour for a little while. What makes antiperspirants more effective is the aluminium compounds: they keep the sweat from actually pouring out of your sweat ducts.

Do antiperspirants cause cancer?

If you thought antiperspirants didn't have it bad enough with all those rumours linking them to Alzheimer's disease, there's also the blow to their reputation ingendered by the claim that they cause breast cancer. Unfortunately, the rumour has at least some substance to it.

The general worry is that antiperspirants contain toxic chemicals that either seep into the skin naturally, even in mere microscopic quantities, or make their way into the body at a comparatively gushing rate through cuts and nicks caused by shaving. The chemicals that get most of the blame are called parabens, a type of preservative that's used not only in deodorants and antiperspirants, but also many foods and pharmaceutical products.

Since parabens have been shown to mimic the activity of oestrogen, and oestrogen is known to fuel the growth of breast cancer cells, many scientists are convinced that exposure to them can increase a person's odds of developing breast cancer. A study of breast cancer tissue in 2004 added fire to that theory when it showed that in a group of samples of tissue taken from human breast tumours, most contained parabens. A second study a year later gave another boost to the theory when it looked at hundreds of breast cancer survivors and found that those who shaved and used antiperspirants the most were diagnosed with breast cancer at the youngest ages.

It all sounds pretty bleak. But before you toss out your razors and deodorant, it's important to point out all the flaws in the research supporting a link.

The paraben study, for example, failed to look at healthy breast tissue or tissues from other parts of the body to confirm that the chemical is found only in cancerous breasts. It also couldn't identify where exactly the parabens came from or whether the women from whom the samples were taken were regular users of antiperspirants. And a large study in the *Journal of the National Cancer Institute* looked at fifteen hundred women and found no relationship between antiperspirants and breast cancer at all. Oh, and women who specifically said they regularly shaved their underarms and then used deodorant or an antiperspirant within an hour of shaving had no increased risk.

Replication is the cornerstone of good science. It's still too early to say whether this claim is bunk, but with only one large study suggesting a link, and another even larger one saying there's none, it's looking as if the claim is on its last legs.

Is artificial light hazardous for your health?

It's long been known that night-shift workers are prone to a range of sleep disorders, including insomnia and trouble staying awake. But when epidemiologists compared people who worked at night with daytime workers several years ago, they found something they weren't expecting: female night-shift workers had elevated rates of breast cancer.

How could that be? What was so dangerous about working at night that it could spark an increase in cancer?

Various explanations were proposed. Socio-economic factors and the stress of burning the midnight oil seemed to be the obvious factors. But after scientists dug a little deeper, they realized that the findings most likely reflected the hazards of constant exposure to artificial light, which disrupts circadian rhythms and throws hormone levels out of whack. Night workers were shown to have chronically low levels of melatonin, a hormone that's switched on by darkness and has been shown to suppress tumour growth. Then a 2004 study by researchers at Brigham and Women's Hospital in Boston and Harvard Medical School found that women who regularly worked night shifts, compared with those who never did, also had significantly higher levels of oestrogen, which can fuel breast cancer.

The same group of researchers also led one of the largest epidemiological studies linking night shifts to breast cancer. That study, published in the *Journal of the National Cancer Institute*, followed more than 78,000 nurses for a decade and found that those who worked the most graveyard shifts were nearly one-and-a-half times more likely to develop breast cancer.

The problem with night-shift work is not the work itself, but that it forces people to spend all day in built-in environments that disrupt the body's internal clock. Up until the twentieth century, most people worked outside, spent all day outside and occasionally slept outside at night. There was no disruption in the dark-light cycle. But now that we have buildings with electric lighting, it's easy to diminish the amplitude of that cycle, and many people — particularly night-shift workers — end up stuck in a sort of architectural jet lag.

At the turn of the nineteenth century, one in thirty women contracted breast cancer. Now the rate is one in eight, and it continues to accelerate at a rate of about 8 per cent a year in industrial societies, even as the rate remains steady in agrarian societies.

Our changing diets and other factors certainly account for some of that, but it can't account for it all. For more answers, I spoke with Dr Mark Rea, the director of the lighting research centre at Rensselaer Polytechnic University Institute in New York, and someone who has been studying the link between artificial light and disease for years. Although unassuming and plain-spoken, Rea is a biophysicist at the head of his field. He said the evidence is still circumstantial but nonetheless strong and building. 'It's clear that all the signs are pointing in the same direction.'

Can air-fresheners hurt your lungs?

Nothing can bring more joy and fresh-eyed wonder than a whiff of spring-breeze-over-golden-meadow-next-to-pine-mountain-scented artificial air-freshener, right?

For a long time, there has been suspicion that a common ingredient in air-fresheners can cause short-term lung problems. That is definitely true. But the good news is that the chemical in question has mostly been phased out of use by the major makers of air-fresheners.

The group of chemicals that cause problems are known as volatile organic compounds, and the one in particular that was used for a long time in air-fresheners is para-dichlorobenzene, or 1,4-DCB. It can also be found in cigarettes, toilet deodorizers and mothballs.

In a study by the National Institutes of Health, Maryland, USA, a team of researchers followed 953 adults for six years and found that people with high blood concentrations of 1,4-DCB had signs of reduced lung function. The 10 per cent of people with the highest blood levels of the chemical, in fact, did 4 per cent worse on tests of lung function than the 10 per cent of people with the lowest levels.

Four per cent may not sound like a lot, but even a small reduction in respiratory function can indicate harm to the lungs. As the level of exposure to 1,4-DCB goes up, so too does the risk of developing asthma.

Some scientists say it makes sense to reduce your exposure to household deodorizers. But the Consumer Specialty Products Association, a trade group, insists that para-dichlorobenzene hasn't been widely used in household products for many years. The products in which it still turns up are urinal blocks, mothballs and hanging deodorizers. It is also found in cheap, generic air-fresheners. Something to keep in mind: any product that contains para-dichlorobenzene should say so on the label.

Do hair dyes cause cancer?

You don't smoke, you avoid pesticides, you stay away from junk food and you won't go anywhere near all sorts of chemicals. But when it comes to covering up those grey hairs or getting a new hair colour, you turn to dye.

With the bad press about potent, carcinogenic chemicals in hair dyes, that might seem like a risk that's not worth taking. But in reality, hair dyes – while not completely risk-free – are not as hazardous as most people have been led to believe. Hair dyes have been popular for at least forty years. For almost just as long, they have also been tarred as toxic. The first concerns were raised in 1975, when a study was published suggesting that a chemical in nearly 90 per cent of permanent hair dyes could cause genetic damage. Facing pressure and criticism, companies voluntarily removed the chemical, a type of coal-tar derivative, but scientists soon identified several other ingredients in hair-dye formulas that also seemed to cause cancer.

Cosmetics companies insist that their formulas have changed in many ways and that hair dyes are completely safe – but that's not completely true.

Several small studies over the years have found higher rates of breast, bladder and other cancers in people who dyed their hair regularly. The most definitive study, however, was published in 2005 in the *Journal of the American Medical Association*. It analyzed seventy-nine previous studies on the subject and found that while hair dye had no effect on the risk of breast and bladder cancers, there was a 'borderline effect' on the risk of developing lymphoma.

Compared to people who had never used hair dye, those who coloured their hair were 1.19 times more likely to get lymphoma, and people who used hair dye before 1980 were about 1.4 times more likely to develop lymphoma. That association, while clearly demonstrating a link, is also considered fairly weak – so weak in fact that most experts and health officials say it does not rise to the level of a public health concern.

Part of the reason for the range of findings may be because the content of hair dyes gradually changed. In any case, there are things you can do to minimize the potential risk that still lurks in the bottle. Dark, permanent dyes are stronger and more concentrated than other colours, so it is best to lower your exposure to them. It also makes sense to wear gloves when applying dye and to paint your hair only up to the edge of the roots, so the product doesn't actually touch your scalp. This might cause your roots to stand out a bit, but isn't it worth the peace of mind?

Does heating or freezing plastic containers expose you to dangerous chemicals?

Water bottles. Tupperware. Takeaway food containers. Plastic straws. Plastic wrap.

If you stop and think about it, the list of plastic things we use to hold or store the things we eat and drink on a daily basis is staggering. Imagine if chemicals in some of these products could leach into your food and poison you. You and everyone you know would be at risk.

So perhaps it shouldn't be a surprise that people panicked when an e-mail hit the Internet warning that heating plastics in the microwave – plastic wrap and Tupperware in particular – can contaminate food with highly toxic chemicals that cause cancer. Another widely circulated e-mail a short time later claimed that freezing or reusing water bottles too frequently could also expose you to the same group of chemicals: dioxins.

'The combination of fat, high heat, and plastics releases dioxins into your food and ultimately into the cells in your body,' stated one such e-mail. 'Saran Wrap placed over foods as they are cooked, with the high heat, actually drips poisonous toxins into the food.'

Dioxins, you might recall, are the same chemicals that were used to poison the Ukrainian president, Viktor Yushchenko, in 2004. He was severely sickened, nearly died and developed a hideously disfiguring facial condition, chloracne, that made him resemble the Toxic Avenger.

Dioxins are some of the most toxic man-made chemicals on Earth. Released into the air largely as by-products of industrial processes, they are ubiquitous, so much so that most living creatures accumulate low levels of them in their bodies. Most

98

exposure occurs through the diet, although trace amounts can be ingested by breathing polluted air.

Plastic wraps and containers can indeed expose you to certain chemicals. But dioxins aren't one of them. In fact, dioxins are almost never found in commercial plastics. If they were, they *could* be liberated by the heat in a microwave and eventually end up in your food, though that wouldn't happen in a plastic water bottle kept at room temperature or in a container that's being frozen because it takes heat for this chemical reaction to get going. In any case, manufacturers don't use them because of the danger.

If there is something worth worrying about, it's a group of chemicals known as phthalates, or plasticizers – the substances that give many plastics their flexibility. While plasticizers can migrate from plastic into food in small amounts, they're not nearly as toxic or deadly as dioxins. There is some evidence from studies linking exposure to plasticizers at high levels to asthma, hormonal problems and other medical conditions. Some scientists also think exposure to plasticizers can increase the risk of developing breast cancer because they can mimic the action of oestrogen, which is known to fuel breast tumours. But the link between plasticizers and cancer, if any, has not been scientifically proven and is widely debated.

In practical terms, it's not clear whether the levels of plasticizers that could get into your food are substantial, and if so whether they pose much of a hazard. But, as Dr Rolf Halden, an expert at the Centre for Water and Health at the Johns Hopkins University, Baltimore, Maryland, put it, 'Why expose yourself to any chemicals you can easily avoid?' Here are some tips you should follow to lower your exposure:

- Only use plastic wrap that says on its packaging that it's intended for microwave use and never let it directly touch your food when heating it.

- Make sure any plastic wrap you use is placed loosely over your food (and be sure to leave one corner open) so that steam can get out. You don't want any droplets that collect on the underside of the wrap to get into your food, since those droplets may contain chemicals from the wrap.

- Never heat any plastic container that does not say on its label or packaging that it's intended for microwave use (this indicates that it's made to withstand high temperatures). Containers that aren't designed *specifically* for use in a microwave can melt or warp, increasing your likelihood of exposure to plasticizers and putting you at risk for spills and burns.

- Things like margarine tubs and takeaway containers from restaurants are not designed to withstand very high temperatures, so never use them in your microwave!

- Don't use any containers that hold prepared microwaveable meals more than once. They are only meant for one-time use.

- It's best to cook in your microwave with pots or containers made from inert materials, like ceramics or heat-resistant glass. It's also OK to use cooking bags, parchment paper and white microwave-safe paper towels.

6
Germs, Germs, Germs

It's a dangerous world out there,
PART II

There is a well-known but puzzling breed of human among us. Theirs is a breed that is obsessed with cleanliness and steering clear of dirt, and we have all seen them.

They're the people who use their elbows to turn on taps, their feet to flush toilets and their forearms to open doors. They use antibacterial soap on an hourly basis and they will not shake hands with anyone. They wash every bed sheet and linen in their closets not once but twice before using them, even when their sheets are brand new.

And they would never – capital N – Never think of eating a piece of food that touched the ground, five-second rule observed or not.

They, of course, are germaphobes. And if their antics don't sound odd to you, it's because you must be one of them.

Not that there is anything wrong with that (OK, maybe just a tad). To some degree, we all have a little germaphobe in us. If our bodies are our temples, as it's often said, then germs are the enemies at the gates.

Some of us may be more vigorous than others when it comes to defending ourselves. But judging by our daily habits, germs are most certainly on our minds all of the time. We use so many antibacterial products that our sewers run rich with them, making it inevitable that one day we will all have to coexist with highly virulent, drug-resistant superbugs, according to the scientists.

And that is only the beginning. Nowadays, you can buy around-the-neck air purifiers, as well as devices that spray disinfectant on doorknobs every twenty minutes. Humans may be social, intimacy-seeking creatures, but at the root of all this germaphobia is some element of fear toward one another. Who knows where that stranger sitting next to you on the bus just came from? So why chance it? Take a seat in the empty row across the aisle.

It is shocking to think that back in the mid-1800s, Louis Pasteur was ridiculed when he first proposed his Germ Theory of Disease. Back then, the cause of sickness was believed to be God's wrath. Microscopic invaders that jumped from one person to the next? Washing your hands and sterilizing medical equipment? Nonsense, people thought; never in a million years.

A century and a half later, it's remarkable how far we've come – or, perhaps, regressed. What's ironic is that sometimes the germs that we spend so much time and effort trying to avoid can do us some good. One emerging theory is that some allergies and chronic diseases are caused by us avoiding germs to such great lengths that our immune systems don't get enough stimulation, preventing them from developing properly. We know from studies, for example, that small children who attend daycare are far less likely to develop asthma than those who don't, precisely because daycare exposes them to more germs early on, which in turn strengthens their immune systems.

In this chapter, we'll delve into some modern-day germ theories to separate myths from facts in order to satisfy that germaphobe in all of us.

Does stepping on something rusty give you tetanus?

It doesn't take an expert on first aid to figure out that getting poked by a rusty nail isn't a great idea. Most ten-year-olds can tell you that you'll risk a tetanus infection. But few people realize that the bacteria that cause tetanus are widespread and that the disease has less to do with the rust than with the nature of the wound.

Clostridia bacteria, the family of C. tetani, can be found in soil, dust, faeces and on the skin. They reproduce only in the absence of oxygen so if a wound's deep enough, it can become a breeding ground.

A rusty nail will do the job. But the infection can come from many sources – sewing needles, tattoo needles, animal bites, gardening tools, even splinters. Injuries that create dead skin, like burns and frostbite, can also lead to an infection.

The symptoms can be severe. Once the bacteria get underneath the skin, they produce toxins that attack the central nervous system, causing spasms and muscle rigidity all over the body, most frequently in the face. The muscle spasms force the body into weirdly contorted, unnatural stretches. Hence the name 'tetanus', derived from the Greek *tetanos*, which means 'to stretch'.

Although the tetanus vaccine is routinely given to children, its effects wear off after ten years, but many people fail to get booster shots. If you come into contact with soil, animals or sharp objects on a regular basis – pretty common stuff for most people – you should make sure to schedule your regular booster. Either that or stay out of the kitchen and away from the playground.

Do toilet seats spread germs?

It's tough to find conventional wisdom that has inspired more dread and disgust than the old claim that public toilet seats are hotbeds of disease and bacteria. Most people won't touch, sit on or go anywhere near public toilets for one reason: 'You never know what you might catch.'

So what do studies have to say about this?

Fortunately – or, on second thoughts, maybe not so fortunately – a lot. First of all, the likelihood of contracting anything from a toilet seat is extremely small. To catch something, the seated party must have a cut or break in the skin that allows a pathogen to enter; intact skin is a surprisingly good barrier against most germs. The other thing is that a sexually transmitted disease most likely wouldn't end up on a toilet seat to begin with, since a person's genitals would have to come into direct contact with the seat. It can happen, but consider the odds.

Now, the bad news. You can definitely get sick from sitting on a bowl that's filthy. The most likely diseases you'll catch: crabs and anything else that's transmitted by skin-to-skin contact. The medical literature is also rife with reports of people catching gonorrhoea and skin infections like pinworm and roundworm. One study in the *New England Journal of Medicine*, for example, found that the bacteria that cause gonorrhoea could survive on a toilet seat for at least two hours.

Viruses that cause sexually transmitted diseases, on the other hand, behave a little differently. Most cannot survive out in the open and in particular they can't make it in the cold, harsh environment that is the toilet seat. Two notable exceptions: hepatitis B, which can survive for a week, and the herpes virus, which can hang on for several hours.

But if you're concerned about toilet seats, you're probably overlooking a more significant hazard. You're far more likely to encounter bacteria and viruses on taps, flush handles and door knobs. Blame that on all those people who don't wash their hands before they leave the bathroom.

Some interesting facts: studies show that women's bathrooms have twice as many germs as men's, mostly because of heavier traffic and nappy-changing facilities. But office work stations are far more contaminated than toilet seats. One study found that because a typical desk is rarely if ever disinfected, it contains an average of four hundred times as many germs as a typical toilet seat. Think about *that* the next time you eat at your desk.

Does antibacterial soap really work better than regular soap?

What ever happened to plain old soap?

Apparently it is fast becoming a relic of the past. Studies show that more than 70 per cent of liquid hand soaps sold in the United States today are labeled antibacterial, and people seem increasingly willing to pay a premium for them. Depending on where you live, some bottles of antibacterial soap can cost more than the cold medications you'd need if you didn't buy soap and did get sick.

But most consumers aren't always getting what they think they are. Over the years, researchers have consistently found that antibacterial soaps are really no better than good old soap and water. At least five studies have confirmed this.

One of them, published in the *Journal of Community Health* in 2003, followed adults in 238 households for nearly a year, all of them in New York City, a town where the levels of dirt and grime are legendary. Month after month, the researchers found no difference in the number of microbes that turned up on the hands of people who used either antibacterial soap or regular soap.

Other studies have found that using antibacterial soaps – and even some of those popular hand-sanitizing gels – won't reduce your likelihood of contracting a cold and other infectious diseases any more than normal soap will.

A large part of the reason for this is simple, but often overlooked: most common infections are caused by viruses, not bacteria.

The only question now, it seems, is whether antibacterial soaps can do more harm than good: many scientists believe they create virulent strains of bacteria that resist antibiotics. And there's the fear that using too many antibacterial products can prevent you from being exposed to routine bacteria, keeping your immune system from bulking up and ultimately increasing your likelihood of getting sick.

Companies that produce antibacterial cleansers insist there is no strong evidence linking their products to the emergence of resistant bacteria, and they argue that their soaps have only limited effects on the environment. In the United States, the US Food and Drug Administration has raised concerns about such products, and in recent years the agency has considered placing restrictions on both how they are used and how they are marketed.

A few sobering facts: according to studies, washing your hands with soap and water reduces your risk of developing diarrhoea by about 45 per cent. It cuts your risk of contracting other severe intestinal infections by as much as 50 per cent. Compared to other parts of your hand, the area beneath your fingernails is home to the most germs and is the most difficult to clean. Artificial fingernails harbour more micro-organisms than natural nails. And the longer your fingernails, the more germs they attract.

Time to take out the nail clippers?

Can toothbrushes spread disease?

Of all the things that people store in their medicine cabinets – pills, razors and, it seems, antibacterial soap – toothbrushes would seem to be the least harmful.

Most dentists would disagree – since toothbrushes are ideal breeding grounds for germs.

Few people realize it, but bacteria actually thrive on toothbrushes, which provide them with ample food and water. And don't forget that toothbrushes sit in one of your home's most germ-laden rooms: the bathroom.

Researchers have found that streptococcus, staphylococcus, influenza and herpes simplex I, among other pathogens, can survive on toothbrushes. No wonder that dentists advise replacing your brush at least every three to four months. But microbes can make it their home long before then.

Bacteria and viruses on one brush can easily spread to another, and sharing your brush with someone else has been shown to cause sickness. All it takes for germs to jump ship and colonize your bristles is setting your toothbrush down next to someone else's.

So where do all these bathroom germs come from? There are several ways your toothbrush can be soiled. A study in the journal *Applied Microbiology* showed that microscopic, bacteria-laden droplets of water that shoot into the air when you flush a toilet can 'remain airborne long enough to settle on surfaces throughout the bathroom'.

Not a very pleasant thought, but good to know.

Today's best oral hygiene advice: skip the medicine cabinet and the bathroom altogether. Bacteria prefer places that are warm, dark and moist – like a cabinet – so one expert who has studied toothbrushes and disease transmission for years, Dr R. Tom Glass, a professor of forensic sciences and dental medicine at Oklahoma State University, recommends keeping your brush out in the open near a bedroom window. Make sure that the toothbrush is propped up vertically, not lying on its back.

And despite the popular belief that motorized brushes are much better for your mouth's health, those attract more germs and can be hard on your gums. Better to use a manual brush with a small, clear head. It's not entirely known why, but translucent and light-coloured heads on toothbrushes seem to harbour lower levels of micro-organisms. This may have something to do with the fact that a clear head allows light, which kills off germs, to pass through it.

Try to replace your toothbrush at least every couple of months. Besides, there's another reason you shouldn't use one toothbrush for too long: people recovering from an illness can easily reinfect themselves by using the same toothbrush.

Can the flu vaccine actually give you a case of the flu?

How cruel a joke it would be if the very vaccine that was meant to protect you from the flu did the reverse. Fortunately, that would never be the case.

It's well known that many people hold out against getting their flu shots each year – including those who need it the most, like seniors and people with chronic medical conditions – because they worry that the virus used to manufacture the vaccine can cause influenza.

Those fears stem in part from a coincidence: because flu vaccines are administered towards the end of the year, some people who get their shots happen to come down with a cold or another respiratory illness that is rampant in the winter. Then there are those unlucky few who get their shots but contract the flu just before their immunity kicks in. All of that can make it seem as if the flu shot can be responsible for a bad case of the flu, when the shot itself isn't to blame.

The two major flu vaccines use dead viruses that are not infectious and can't make you sick. A newer version of the vaccine, a nasal spray called FluMist, uses live but weakened viruses, so it's not recommended for the elderly, anyone with a chronic medical condition, or people with lowered immunity. People who use it can give off the disabled live virus, though this hasn't been shown to cause sickness in other people.

Health officials like to say that the spray is a boon because it can fill a void during shortages of the normal vaccine. But let's be honest, it's really for those of us who consider the pain of a needle injection a fate worse than death and for those of us who think buying the spray at a pharmacy sounds simpler than going to a doctor's office for a needle. (Come to think of it, that might be just about everyone.)

Although the vaccine won't give you the flu, it can cause some side effects – a sore arm, obviously, and in a small percentage of people, mild illness. 'But if you put it in perspective, it's still nothing compared to the real flu,' said Dr James C. King Jr., a vaccine expert at the University of Maryland, USA.

King has good reason to persuade people to get their shots: he was the author of a study a few years back that found that vaccinating your children can save you money. That's because young children – bless their little hearts – are germ magnets, who sit in germ-infested classrooms and run around in germ-infested playgrounds all day. Vaccinating them makes it less likely that they'll contract flu from playmates and then bring it home to you, the adult. That results in fewer workdays lost to sickness, less money spent on flu medications and fewer visits to the doctor.

There's also all the money you'll save by not having to pay for all those ridiculously overpriced boxes of tissues.

Can dead bodies after a disaster start an epidemic?

In most parts of the world, after natural disasters inflict enormous casualties, a grim and predictable chain of events takes hold. The sight and stench of dead bodies set off fears of an impending epidemic. That in turn prompts local health officials to call for remains to be buried as quickly as possible – sometimes in mass graves and without identifying them first – a drastic measure that only compounds grief for the victims' relatives. This terror emerged after the tsunami that swept through the Asian Pacific in 2004 took hundreds of thousands of lives, after Hurricane Jeanne killed two thousand people in Haiti the same year and Hurricane Katrina ravaged New Orleans in 2005, and after major earthquakes shook El Salvador in 2001 and Turkey in 2003.

Yet, the risk of cadavers giving rise to an epidemic after a natural disaster is really negligible.

Oliver Morgan, a researcher who published a study on the phenomenon in the *Pan American Journal of Public Health* in 2004, said that large-scale disasters and outbreaks of infectious diseases have sometimes occurred together by coincidence, leading many people to suspect the dead were to blame.

But only dead bodies that are infected with a disease can spread it. Disaster victims pose little threat because they have usually died from trauma, not infections.

A contagious disease that is present before death can be transmitted to people handling the cadaver for roughly a couple of days, depending on the pathogen. Mortuary and emergency workers are at greatest risk, though the danger decreases if protective gloves, gowns and masks are worn.

Is it true that pregnant women should stay away from cats?

Most pregnant women know they should steer clear of things that can affect their babies. Since the 1970s, alcohol and cigarettes have become a no-brainer. Even caffeine is generally considered out of the question. But cats?

It sounds ridiculous, potentially just another reason for some of us to be dog lovers. But expectant mothers are often told that their cats are a potential threat. It's a warning that has the ring of an old wives' tale or witches' brew, like the scare about cats smothering babies and sucking the air out of them. (Note: there

are no documented cases of this happening.) But this one has to do with the feline ability to carry *Toxoplasma gondii*, a parasite that causes birth defects and miscarriages.

Cats usually contract toxoplasma by eating small prey that already harbour the parasite, which makes the condition rare among indoor-only cats. But they can also get it by eating contaminated raw meat – particularly cold cuts – and so can humans.

Once a cat is infected, it sheds the organism in its droppings, which can infect anyone who comes into contact with them. Expectant mothers are most vulnerable. Roughly three thousand women transmit the infection to their foetuses every year and a small percentage of newborns are born with serious damage as a result.

But pregnant women don't necessarily have to banish their cats. There are ways to keep Felix and still limit your risk: avoid litter boxes, cover any outdoor sandboxes and wear gloves while gardening to minimize contact with droppings. Better to have a friend or relative maintain the litter box instead.

Then once the baby is born, Felix can welcome it with open paws.

Is a cold contagious before your symptoms emerge?

The signs are unmistakable. A fit of sneezing, a sore throat, stuffy congestion so miserable that seemingly no amount of tissues can help.

Anyone can spot the onset of a winter cold, but most people don't know when a person who has picked up the virus actually becomes contagious or for how long.

The common cold – like chickenpox, measles and many other viral diseases – can be spread before and after symptoms emerge. The time between infection and signs of illness, or the incubation period, is about three to five days for most viral diseases, but colds move a little faster.

One expert, Dr Daniel J. Skiest, the associate chief of clinical infectious diseases at the University of Texas Southwestern Medical Centre, points out that more than two hundred different viruses are known to cause colds. Depending on which strain you contract, you can become contagious roughly a day after infection, even though symptoms won't appear, on average, until another day or two later.

When obvious signs of sickness have disappeared, you can still infect others for up to three days. That means no one can entirely keep from catching colds by steering clear of people with symptoms, though it helps.

So what can you do to cut your chances of getting sick? The most important step is avoiding crowds, particularly during the peak cold seasons of September, January and April. Avoid rubbing your eyes and your nose and wash your hands as often as you can (and as you know, plain old soap is fine). That's because colds are transmitted mainly through infected droplets in the air and through virus particles transferred from nose to hand to someone else's hand. If you don't want to look like a lunatic who runs to the bathroom twenty times a day, then limit your hand washing to before meals, before and after you use the bathroom and after taking public transportation – those are the most essential times.

About a third of all colds are caused by rhinoviruses, which are spread best in those horrifying droplets coming from a runny nose or through sprays of droplets from coughs and sneezes.

Remember that advice from your parents about covering your mouth and nose when you cough or sneeze? Take it.

Will you get more sick if you exercise while you have a cold?

People who exercise regularly suffer fewer colds than those who avoid the gym at all costs; that much is known. But some people argue that once you do get sick, a little exercise can speed your recovery by bolstering your immune system, while others swear it has the opposite effect, taxing a weak body and prolonging misery.

But both camps are wrong.

Scientists who have examined the question have repeatedly found that there is no effect, and in interesting ways. Most studies have been conducted by recruiting human guinea pigs (read: skint university students) and infecting them with a rhinovirus (the usual cause of a cold), before examining how their bodies react to exercise.

In one experiment, carried out in 1998, a team of researchers injected a group of fifty students with a rhinovirus, and then had part of the group run, climb stairs or cycle at moderate intensity for forty minutes every other day, while the second group remained relatively sedentary.

And in an unpleasant and slightly disturbing measure of just how far these researchers were willing to go in the name of science, they collected and weighed the subjects' used facial tissues. Which raises a small question: which group could have possibly had it any worse in this study – the students who signed up to be infected with someone else's germs, or the researchers who were forced to pick up their discarded tissues and 'analyze' them?

That, unfortunately, is one thing the study didn't answer. But what it did determine was this: after ten days, the exercise regimen neither eased nor worsened symptoms of the common cold. Nor did it affect duration. Several similar studies conducted elsewhere have found the same thing.

But not everyone is convinced. Dr Marc Siegel, an associate professor of medicine at New York University, said that exercise should have a beneficial effect because it increases the activity of white blood cells. If there is an effect, though, it's probably too small to notice.

When it comes to exercising with a cold, there's a good rule of thumb. Doctors refer to it as the 'neck check'. It's safe to exercise if you have only 'above the neck' symptoms, like a runny nose, sneezing or a scratchy throat. If your symptoms are 'below the neck' – a fever, nausea, or diarrhoea – you're better off sitting it out for a few days.

7
Mother's Medicine
Patient, heal thyself

You are suffering miserably from a cold that won't go away, but you aren't planning on seeing a doctor over a case of the sniffles. You have a nasty gash on your arm that needs a bandage and some ointment, but it's nothing too serious. A toothache has been irritating you for two days, but wasting a sick day to see a dentist is not an option.

These are the times that call for creativity. These are the times when we scrounge around the house in desperation, the times when we dig deep inside the medicine cabinet, rifle through the kitchen and scan through our mental archive of useful things we learned when we were young, hoping to come up with the right cure for that annoying ailment.

Thankfully, there are remedies that occupy the category just below medical intervention and just above medical quackery. Some of us swear by them, most of us repeat them. There is whisky for a toothache, cranberry juice for urinary infections and chicken soup for a cold (and, it seems, the soul). And without a doubt, many household remedies have been around for centuries. After all, what else did we have to rely on before the dawn of prescription drugs and penicillin?

Home remedies have a long history. But they have also had their detractors. At the turn of the last century, as vaccines and new technology helped facilitate the emergence of modern medicine, medical authorities began to question any treatment that couldn't be obtained through a doctor. Take, for example, the following letter from a doctor that was published in *The New York Times* in 1913.

'Every medicine is poisonous unless judiciously employed, and the lay consumer is incapable of quantitative and qualitative analysis, and some of them lay their lives on the altar of ignorance. The employment of so-called household remedies,' he goes on, 'must be very extensive because a department store catering largely to poor people recently advertised a bargain sale of medicine cabinets – a most dangerous possession of the ignorant.'

Obviously that view is a tad outdated. But it raises a good question. Which well-known, time-honoured remedies can we put our faith in and which ones can we cast into the waste bin of useless antidotes?

In the next few pages, we'll explore the science behind a variety of claims about self-medicating in the hopes of proving or disputing them – including, of course, the big one: whether taking echinacea can do anything for a cold.

Can echinacea really help you beat a cold?

It's the crown jewel of herbal medicine, the gold standard that millions swear by. Unfortunately, the science is pretty clear on this one, and echinacea, despite decades of anecdotal evidence to the contrary, will not help you kick a cold once it's already started. When it comes to whether or not taking it can help ward off colds later on, though, the jury is still out.

It is safe to say that no herbal medicine has been studied as closely as echinacea, mostly because it has such a long history as a natural panacea. Derived from the purple coneflower, echinacea was used by Native Americans for all sorts of conditions – coughs, sore mouth, hydrophobia, even snakebites. There is probably no condition that someone, somewhere, hasn't tried using it to cure or alleviate. But its reputation as a cold cure can be traced back to the early twentieth century, when it gained ground in Germany as a treatment for respiratory illness. Word spread gradually. Fast forward to today, and you can't walk into any health food store without seeing it sold as a cure for the cold or the flu.

Dozens of studies have examined whether it can actually do what everyone says, and every one of the most thorough studies has failed to endorse it. Among the largest and most rigorous, a 2005 study published in the *New England Journal of Medicine* involved 437 people who volunteered to have cold viruses dripped into their noses. Some took echinacea in three hundred milligram doses for a week beforehand (the dose most often used by consumers), some were given a placebo and others were given either echinacea or the placebo at the time they were infected.

For five days, the subjects were secluded in a hotel and examined closely. The echinacea groups were just as likely to catch a cold as the others. They showed no difference in symptoms, no difference in viral secretions and no increases in their levels of interleukin-8, an immune system protein that many people believed was the mechanism behind echinacea's curative powers.

There goes that theory.

But that study and others clearly haven't done much to knock echinacea off its pedestal. Companies are still marketing it as a cure for the cold and few people have been clearing their medicine cabinets of echinacea bottles.

And they probably shouldn't. Some scientists say we could use more studies that look, for example, at taking the herb in larger doses, smaller doses and different forms before we close the book. There's also some evidence from the decades of research on echinacea that people who take it for long periods of time in small doses – not just when they get a cold, or a week before they get a cold, but for months or years – get sick less often.

Do wounds heal better when they're allowed to breathe and scab over?

Most parents and school nurses have a time-honoured approach to treating the small cuts and scrapes that a harsh world can inflict upon a child's skin: clean up the wound, stop the bleeding, then let it get some air. And never, ever pick at the scab, no matter how much it itches or raises its ugly crust.

The point of this approach, as described in medical texts, is to lower the odds of infection and to speed the healing process. That, we have been told, is the safest and most effective route to recovery.

But researchers and dermatologists have discovered that what many people know about treating small cuts and scrapes is incorrect. Your school nurse was wrong. Your parents were wrong. That boy who sat in the back of your class and picked at his scabs – he, of all people, was right.

Exposing a wound to the air so it can breathe is a terrible mistake, it turns out, because it creates a dry environment that promotes cell death.

A handful of studies have found that when wounds are kept moist and covered, blood vessels regenerate faster and the number of cells that cause inflammation drop more rapidly than they do in wounds allowed to air out. Today's best medical advice: it is best to keep a wound moist and covered for at least five days.

A plaster, it is worth noting, can do several things. It wards off infection, keeps the wound moist and protects the area from sunlight, which stimulates the production of pigment and can cause discolouration.

Another common mistake people make is applying antibiotic ointments. These ointments may keep the wound moist, but they can also lead to swelling and an allergic reaction called contact dermatitis. Plain and simple Vaseline, applied twice a day, works fine.

And yes, you can go ahead and pick away at that unsightly scab when no one is watching: a small initial scab will help stop the bleeding, but if left for too long it will leave a larger scar. The best way to remove the scab is to soak and slowly remove it, then dry the area and slather on some Vaseline.

'You don't want the scab to mature too much because it increases scarring,' said Dr Mark D. P. Davis, a professor of dermatology who deals with scabs and tender skin all the time. 'That's the general thinking.'

Is it true you should never let a person with a head injury fall asleep?

There's an old story about Cher that comes to mind when thinking about this question. Legend has it that back in the 1970s, when Cher was engaged to legendary rocker, party animal, and founding member of the Allman Brothers band Gregg Allman, she spent an entire night walking him around after a near-fatal drug overdose. Supposedly her intention was to keep him awake so he wouldn't slip into a coma.

I don't know anyone that can relate to that particular scenario. But it illustrates the fact that many people think they can keep a person from slipping into a deadly coma by shaking them around and telling them not to head toward the light. It's well known that right after people suffer head injuries or anything that alters consciousness, those around them should force them to stay awake until help arrives, abiding by the old wives' tale that says that being awake lowers your risk of lapsing into a coma and possibly worse.

Seems like common sense: what if the person falls asleep and never wakes up? As long as they are kept awake, you can be sure you haven't lost them. But it's a belief that doctors say is rooted in a misconception.

When a person suffers a traumatic blow to the head, their brain usually bruises and swells, often leading to a cluster of symptoms – brief unconsciousness, light-headedness, nausea – that we call a concussion. Usually the symptoms clear up over the course of a few days and there is no permanent damage. Only when the person suffers bleeding inside their head, which is rare, is there a serious risk of death.

Dr Philip Stieg, the chairman of neurosurgery at New York Presbyterian/Weill Cornell Hospital, explained that the fear that a person who suffers a concussion or altered consciousness might fall asleep and never wake up stems from a phenomenon known as the lucid interval, in which a person seems coherent shortly after being knocked out but later slips into a coma and dies.

That's something that doesn't happen often. One study in 2005 looked at hundreds of children who were examined after suffering head injuries that later turned fatal and found that only 2 per cent had been declared lucid by doctors before they died. Five of those six, the researchers found, were infants whose skills most likely hadn't developed enough to be assessed accurately.

A good rule, neurologists say, is that unconsciousness is serious. When someone is knocked out and then comes to and seems drowsy, sleep is immaterial. You can grab them by the shoulders and tell them to stay awake, but it won't do any good. At that point, only medical attention can make a difference.

Does drinking cranberry juice prevent urinary tract infections?

Centuries before the first vodka cocktail was invented, cranberry juice had already made a name for itself – as medicine. Native Americans extolled its curative powers over a variety of infections as early as the 1600s. Often they would brew cranberry poultices and use them to treat the poison in arrow wounds. Cranberries were an antibiotic of sorts.

Turns out the Native Americans were on to something. In the last two decades, scientists have documented that cranberries contain a host of antibacterial properties, capable of preventing a variety of infections, chief among them UTIs. How anyone figured this out long before science could prove it is anyone's guess, but it comes down to the compounds in berries.

A study, published in the *New England Journal of Medicine* in 1998, showed that cranberries (and blueberries) contain proanthocyanidin, a substance that prevents E. coli from adhering to cells that line the urinary tract. Three years later, another study, published in the medical journal *BMJ*, found that women who drank cranberry juice every day for six months had a far lower risk of urinary tract infections than those in a control group. Six months after they ended their daily regimen, the women in the cranberry group still had a lower risk, suggesting there were long-term benefits.

But there are some limitations. Not only does it take at least two glasses of cranberry juice a day to produce an effect, but people at extremely high risk of infections, like those with bladder disease, see no benefit. And while cranberry juice has preventive powers, there's no evidence that it can clear up infections once they begin. When that happens, you'll have to turn to more modern-day antibiotics, like amoxicillin or ampicillin.

Can drinking green tea lower your risk of getting cancer?

It has been called an herbal panacea, able to help you lose weight, lower your cholesterol and generally safeguard your health. Health food stores have been selling the stuff as a heart-healthy brew for decades. And even soft-drink makers have jumped on the bandwagon and are now selling it as a sugary and purportedly healthy drink.

But when it comes to one of the most cited benefits of drinking green tea, its ability to fight a slew of cancers, studies have found plenty of promise and not a lot of evidence.

The promise stems from the tea's polyphenols – powerful antioxidants that studies have shown can inhibit the growth of cancer cells in animals. But the evidence has been lacking when researchers have tried to determine if the findings carry over into humans. Results so far – at the very best – are really no better than mixed.

So what do we know? A 2001 study in the *New England Journal of Medicine* followed tens of thousands of people in Japan for eight years and found no connection between how much green tea they drank and their rates of stomach cancer, which is the most common cancer in Japan. Then, in 2004, a study of breast cancer in more than thirty-five thousand Japanese women had similar findings.

But the cancer studies haven't all been bad for green tea. To be fair, there have been some that favoured it. One study in

Los Angeles in 2003 found drastically lower rates of breast cancer among women who drank the bitter brew on a regular basis. And two other studies in China, where green tea is a dietary staple, found that green-tea drinkers had lower rates of stomach cancer, oesophageal cancer, and pre-cancerous oral plaques. One of those studies found that it took little more than two cups of green tea a day to see an effect (many people drink that much coffee without even blinking). But the truth is that there have been far more studies like the ones in Japan, which found no effect, than the studies in China and Los Angeles.

But if you're a green-tea drinker, don't fear. You won't do any harm by drinking the stuff. If a day comes when green tea is proven as a cancer fighter, and you're one of those health fanatics who imbibe the stuff like water, you'll be happy you did. And if it never pans out, well, no harm done. What doesn't prevent cancer only makes you stronger (or something like that, right?).

Can raisins soaked in gin cure arthritis?

Not surprisingly, there haven't been any rigorous clinical studies proving the efficacy of gin-soaked raisins as a remedy for arthritic pain. But there is some circumstantial evidence for its effectiveness. Studies have shown, for example, that a group of compounds in grapes and raisins called proanthocyanidins have potent anti-inflammatory properties, and that they also seek out and fight free radicals and other disease-causing substances in the body. Arthritis, of course, is a condition characterized by inflammation.

Raisins also contain sulphur, which in its naturally occurring form is used as a pain-relieving supplement among arthritis sufferers.

Dr Steven Abramson, the director of rheumatology at the New York University Hospital for Joint Diseases, said he hears the gin-soaked raisin claim from his patients all the time and thinks there may be something to it. It may have to do with resveratrol, the powerful antioxidant that gives red wine many of its health properties, he noted.

'We've been looking at what's in red wine and trying to find out what it can do for joint disease,' he said. 'My own lab work says that maybe there is something in grapes and raisins that can help arthritis – and a little gin to cure the pain can't be all that bad.'

Hmm. Well, there is a small hitch. Resveratrol is found only in the skin of red grapes, so the remedy would not be found in white or golden raisins, which come from white grapes.

No rheumatologist would endorse gin-soaked raisins as a proven treatment, since as of now (without the studies), it simply isn't. But Abramson said that for those looking for a safer alternative medicine than the bottles of herbal pills at the local health food shop, this might be an option worth trying.

Then again, a trip to the local off-licence might also do the trick.

'If I'm looking for the active antioxidant in grapes, I'd rather drink red wine than eat raisins,' Abramson joked. 'But that's just me. People have different preferences.'

Can a shot of whisky cure a toothache?

If a little gin or whisky can ease the mind or dull the senses, then why not use it on a toothache? A lot of people, in fact, do just that, heeding the old-fashioned advice that a strong drink rubbed on the gums, swished in the mouth or knocked straight back can bring relief from dental distress.

It's a practice that's been swirling around for a long time. Before the dawn of modern medical and dental care, there was no such thing as anaesthesia and certainly nothing at all like penicillin. Those were the days when a set of pliers and a good bottle of bourbon were part of every dental kit.

Nowadays, we have prescription drugs and operating rooms to get us through our serious ailments. When in a tight spot, a good swig of whisky will still conquer pain. But most people who turn to Dr Jack Daniels for a toothache are probably thinking that the alcohol content will act as a potent antiseptic, killing off bacteria and clearing up any infection. Take a swig, swoosh a bit, close the bottle and forget about it. No needles, and no one poking around in your mouth with those starchy latex gloves.

But don't kid yourself. Alcohol does have some ability to fight bacteria, but not much. It's not going to clear up an infection in the mouth, and it doesn't have any value as a local anaesthetic.

The other problem is that a minor toothache can be an early sign of a much larger problem that requires dental care.

It could mean there's decay in one of your molars. Or it could mean the pulp of your tooth and the gums around it are seriously infected. Point is, delaying treatment can worsen the outcome.

As Dr Matthew J. Messina, a spokesman for the American Dental Association, told me, only a dentist can figure out what's going on for sure.

'The people that are looking for this kind of quick remedy are often afraid to go to the dentist,' he said. 'But the other side to that is that the longer you wait, the more it ties my hands. If we deal with it now, when it's simple, then it's an easier situation.'

In other words, get it over with. Don't wait until the problem is magnified. In many cases, a toothache calls for an antibiotic. But when it's the middle of the night and the pain is unbearable, or a teething baby needs some relief, then over-the-counter pain medication can ease the suffering until the next morning. Keep the whisky around for better uses.

Is there an easy way to diagnose if someone has had a stroke?

It doesn't take much to spot the telltale signs of a heart attack. But a stroke?

That's far more difficult. So difficult, in fact, that stroke victims themselves often fail to realize that they've suffered one. Studies show that in many cases, stroke victims – not realizing their condition – neglect to seek medical help until crucial hours later. Minor strokes, for example, are often dismissed as migraines or fatigue.

So when an e-mail message – that modern version of the old wives' tale – claiming that anyone can diagnose a stroke in three simple steps surfaced, it was tantalizing. And why not? Many people take CPR classes every year so they can be helpful in an emergency. Learning to diagnose a stroke quickly and effectively could be just as useful.

Besides, the message starts persuasively, with a compelling story about a woman, named Susie, who survives a massive stroke that could have killed her, all because her good friend Sherry had read up on the amazing three-step stroke test and knew to administer it at the right time.

Sherry, the message explains, knew to ask Susie to do three easy-to-remember things: smile, raise both of her arms slowly and recite a simple sentence. If a person cannot do any one of the three, the person fails the test and must seek immediate medical attention for a stroke. If they can do all three, then all's well.

Most chain e-mails like this cite a bogus study or fictitious doctor. But this one was no sham. The message credited the test to a small study presented at a meeting of the American Stroke Association in 2003. The ASA subsequently came out and said that it did not endorse the test.

The symptoms of a stroke can vary widely, which means that the three-step test will detect some victims and miss many others. One of the test's detractors, Dr Larry Goldstein, points out that some of the most common symptoms of a stroke are problems seeing, an unusual headache, sudden numbness, and trouble with coordination or walking – symptoms that are all excluded from the three-step test.

Having someone take the three-step test to check whether they had a stroke is like having someone read a billboard to determine whether his eyesight is weak. Even if you pass the test, it doesn't mean you're fine.

'The danger is that someone can have abrupt changes in their neurological capabilities that are dismissed because they aren't one of those three things in the test,' Goldstein warned. In reality, if you suspect someone has suffered a stroke, quick medical treatment, not a three-step test, is the only thing that can help.

Can taking antioxidants keep your heart healthy?

In the early 1980s, scientists who study heart disease discovered something that seemed like a breakthrough.

The countries that had the highest rates of the disease, they noticed, also tended to be deficient in selenium, a photosensitive trace element with potent antioxidant properties. No country seemed to illustrate this more clearly than Finland, where studies of tens of thousands of citizens concluded that low dietary levels of selenium were to blame for about 22 per cent of the nation's deaths from heart attacks.

One region of Finland, a cold, rural area that straddles the border of Russia, called North Karelia, had the highest mortality rate from heart disease in the world. It was seen as no coincidence that people there had some of the lowest levels of selenium in their blood systems as well.

News of the possible connection between selenium and heart disease led to widespread claims that taking selenium supplements might ward off heart disease or perhaps treat it. It even prompted lawmakers in Finland to enact legislation requiring that selenium be added to soil and crops, and led to similar efforts by health officials and legislators in other countries.

But now, two decades later, it's looking more and more as though selenium's power was overstated, and those of us who keep a bottle of the stuff in our medicine cabinets might need to reconsider. Various studies have chipped away at the assertion that selenium has any ability to fight heart disease. A large study published in the *American Journal of Epidemiology* in 2006 appears to deliver the final blow.

The study followed more than a thousand adults for seven and a half years, some of whom took two hundred micrograms of selenium daily and others who were assigned placebos. After taking blood samples twice a year, and controlling for health habits, background and other factors, it was clear to the researchers that selenium had no effect on the risk of developing heart disease or of dying from it. And there's more. Other studies have found that even combining selenium with other antioxidant supplements, like vitamin E, has little or no effect on heart disease.

But the news hasn't all been negative. Studies have found that people who take selenium have lower rates of colorectal, prostate and lung cancer than their peers who don't. The findings are widely debated, but they certainly hold promise.

As for those weak-hearted Finns over in North Karelia – which most of us know today as Nokia country – ever since selenium was added to their soil, the rates of people dying from heart disease have plummeted. But most scientists think that has more to do with the massive, unprecedented health awareness campaign that Finnish health officials launched in the 1970s and continued through to the 1990s.

The campaign encouraged people to cut back on their extraordinarily high consumption of saturated fats, salt, meat and sugar, and to add more fruits and vegetables to their meals, which typically had consisted of sausages and high-fat dairy products. As one health official at the time pointed out in the publication *New Scientist*, before the health campaign, most Finns considered anything green 'animal food'.

Can you keep yourself alive during a heart attack by coughing?

Many people know how to perform CPR in an emergency to save someone who slips into cardiac arrest. But what if *you* are the one in need of CPR and there's no one around to perform it?

'What can you do?' a widely circulated (and unsigned) e-mail message asked. 'You've been trained in CPR, but the guy who taught the course neglected to tell you how to perform it on yourself.'

According to the e-mail, if you feel the radiating chest pains and light-headedness that often signal a heart attack, you can keep yourself conscious by breathing deeply and coughing vigorously. This supposedly increases oxygen levels and squeezes the heart, allowing blood to circulate. 'The squeezing pressure on the heart also helps it regain normal rhythm,' the message claimed. 'In this way, heart attack victims can get to a phone and, between breaths, call for help.'

But don't buy it. Like most of the tantalizing medical advice that's dispensed through e-mails that never seem to stop ricocheting in and out of inboxes, the notion that you can slow the progression of a heart attack by coughing is bogus. If anything, it'll do more harm than good.

Whoever started this may have confused it with the fact that people having angiograms are sometimes asked to cough forcefully when they have sudden abnormal heartbeats. True, coughing deeply can help a person who is on the verge of passing out – a sign of cardiac arrest – maintain consciousness until treatment can be administered.

But this is so dangerous it's only done while a person is under medical supervision. And for someone having a heart attack that does not result in cardiac arrest, coughing can actually accelerate the attack and delay treatment. Since the average person can't tell the difference, cardiac experts strongly encourage people not to try this technique, at home or anywhere else (except, of course, the hospital, if your doctor prescribes it).

One small aside: a study published in 1998 did find that the technique could be useful for people who suffer from a rare condition known as Stokes-Adams syndrome, which causes heart arrhythmias and frequent fainting. But in typical cases, it's best to stick to a tried-and-tested technique: call for help and take an aspirin quickly.

Are those white spots on your fingernails a sign that you need more calcium?

As I'm writing this, a half-empty bottle of calcium pills is staring up at me from my desk. About fifteen years ago, when I first noticed white dots on my fingernails and began to wonder about them, my older brother convinced me they were a sign of calcium deficiency. Where he got this from I have no idea, but it seems to be a common belief. I bought it, and thanks to him, I've gone through life thinking I could use more calcium in my diet.

It wasn't until I sifted through the scientific literature in a burst of self-serving reporting (how much more milk can a body need?) that I realized I'd been duped. But it turns out that a lot of people have glanced down at their fingernails on occasion and wondered why there was a smattering of white freckles. The phenomenon is common enough that dermatologists have a grim name for it that, in keeping with the medical tradition, is also unpronounceable: *punctate leukonychia*. Translation: 'white spots'.

So what are those things? More often than not, leukonychia is caused by mild trauma to the base of the nail plate, usually from a hard knock or blow to the fingers. Getting your digits crunched in a car door will do it nearly every time. A rough manicure that puts a lot of pressure on the nails, an allergic reaction to enamels, and bacterial and fungal infections can also be the culprit. The fact that accidents and manicures are frequent causes might explain why the spots are most commonly seen in women and children (two groups who are also quite prone to the calcium anxieties).

The white colour that you see is usually one of two things: trapped air or a structural defect in the nail itself. It takes more than eight months for a fingernail to grow out, so if you see a white spot halfway up your nail, it means the damage occurred within the last four months.

But these spots are not exclusive to fingernails. They can also appear on toes, something runners whose feet take a beating have probably noticed. Although the spots are usually harmless, they can be a sign of one of several serious conditions, particularly if the nail turns completely white. Among the conditions the spots can signal are liver disease, typhoid fever, zinc deficiency and gout.

But if you did have one of these conditions, you'd probably know it long before any white spots showed up.

Does drinking milk make you phlegmy?

Now that I think about it, maybe my older brother was pulling my leg. Because around the tender age of six, he also instilled in me a deep suspiciousness toward milk – the exact thing that was supposed to cure my white spots. He advised me that drinking milk would make me produce more mucus and that drinking too much could make me choke on my own phlegm.

He was wrong about that last part.

But what about the first part? Most people have been taught since childhood that milk causes excess mucus and as a result should always be avoided during a cold, especially when it comes to asthmatics. In fact, the belief that milk ramps up mucus production dates back to the twelfth century's legendary rabbi, philosopher and physician Moses Maimonides, who wrote about it in his bestselling book, *Treatise on Asthma*. Maimonides was a chap with a lot of foresight. In the same book, he advocated a quick home remedy for colds that you might have heard of: chicken soup. (That's coming up next.)

Repeated by generations of parents and older brothers alike, the milk-mucus link is now considered conventional wisdom. But it's also plain wrong. A look at the science shows that the connection is mostly an illusion. What can seem like an increase in mucus after drinking milk is just a slight thickening of your saliva.

In a dogged and slightly bizarre quest to get to the bottom of this myth, a heroic team of Australian researchers carried out a study in which they weighed the nasal secretions of dozens of people who volunteered to have cold viruses squirted up their noses. For ten days, the scientists followed the subjects, keeping track of how much milk they drank and how much mucus they produced. They found no connection between milk intake, nasal secretions and congestion.

But like any great question facing scientists, it could not be settled with just one study. So along came another team who decided to compare mucus production in different people after they drank either a glass of milk or a non-dairy placebo that was made to taste like milk. In each case, there was no difference in mucus production. Other studies that examined whether asthmatics or people suffering from a cold produce more mucus after a glass of milk also found no difference.

Dr Allen J. Dozor, a grizzled asthma researcher who, in his

first line of work as a paediatrician, has probably had to face all kinds of icky secretions, said it's clear there's nothing to the claim. For the extremely small percentage of people with an allergy to the protein in cow's milk, there's a slight possibility that drinking milk could increase mucus. But for most of us, milk has no effect, and there's no need to cut back on it during a cold or an illness – unless, of course, you take yours in the form of a White Russian.

Is chicken soup really good for a cold?

Mothers have been serving warm bowls of chicken soup to sniffling kids ever since Maimonides proclaimed that a nice bowl was 'very good for you, but bad for the chicken'. But Maimonides was wrong about milk and mucus, so how does the chicken-soup cure stand up after eight hundred years?

As it happens, for just about as long as the claim has been circulating, scientists have been struggling to determine whether mothers and Maimonides were right. In their quest for scientific truth, scientists, microscopes in hand, have studied various brands of soup, analyzed countless concoctions, looked at their effects on brave but sickly volunteers, and even tried to come up with the perfect cold-fighting recipe for chicken soup. And so far they have all reached the same conclusion: chicken soup works.

In 1978, scientists at the Mount Sinai Medical Centre in Miami Beach, USA, published a study that found that eating chicken soup cleared up congestion and stuffiness better than hot or cold water. They worked this out after first noticing that a signature symptom of colds, the runny nose, isn't caused by the cold virus per se, but by the immune system. A runny nose is the body's way of removing invaders; it's our first line of defence. So the scientists decided that by measuring 'nasal mucus velocity', they could determine the effectiveness of various treatments: a greater mucus velocity (i.e. pathogen removal) meant a more effective treatment.

The scientists found that volunteers who drank hot water had a greater increase in velocity than volunteers who drank cold water, and that chicken-soup imbibers had the greatest increase of all. Further proof came years later when other scientists showed that the protein in chicken contains an amino acid called cysteine. Cysteine, it turns out, is chemically similar to acetylcysteine, a medicine that dissolves mucus in the lungs, allowing it to be coughed up more easily.

In 2000, a group of scientists set out to show not only that chicken soup could ease a cold (replication, as it's said, being the source of good science), but also to discover precisely which brands and varieties of chicken soup work best. If that weren't comedic enough for such a serious scientific endeavour, the results of which were published in the prominent journal *Chest*, the scientists also provided a detailed recipe for the soup they used.

In the study, they tested nineteen samples of this particular soup recipe, and found in laboratory tests that it suppressed inflammatory white cells (neutrophils) that produce coughing, congestion, malaise and other symptoms of the common cold. Better yet, the soup worked even after it was diluted a lot.

'The present study,' the scientists wrote, 'suggests that chicken soup may contain a number of substances with beneficial medicinal activity. A mild anti-inflammatory effect could be one mechanism by which the soup could result in the mitigation of symptomatic upper respiratory tract infections.'

They tested some other shop-bought soups, too, about a dozen altogether. All but one had cold-fighting powers. Campbell's worked fine, as did Lipton and plenty of other brands. The one exception: chicken-flavoured ramen noodles.

Big surprise.

But more importantly, they provided this proven home recipe (the one tested in the study), which came from Celia Fleischer, the grandmother of one of the study's authors.

So here you have it, the first scientifically vetted recipe for chicken soup. It only took about a millennium of scientific conjecture and experiments to produce. Enjoy.

1 5- to 6-lb stewing hen or baking chicken
1 package of chicken wings
3 large onions
1 large sweet potato
3 parsnips
2 turnips
11 or 12 large carrots
5 or 6 celery stems

1 bunch of parsley
salt and pepper to taste

Add the chicken to a large pot with cold water and bring to the boil. Add the chicken wings, onions, sweet potato, parsnips, turnips and carrots. Boil for about 90 minutes, removing fat from the surface as it accumulates. Add the parsley and celery. Cook the mixture about forty-five minutes longer. Remove the chicken, which is no longer needed for the soup. (The meat makes excellent chicken parmesan.) Put the vegetables in a food processor until they are chopped fine or pass through a strainer. Add salt and pepper to taste.

Feed to sniffling toddler.

8
Bad Habits

Stressed out over the small (and big) stuff

If there's one trait that must be common to children everywhere, it's the bad habit. You may have bitten your fingernails, picked your nose or sucked on your thumb. But chances are that as a kid you did something that you weren't supposed to – not only day in and day out, but multiple times a day.

And if you're like me, the only thing that broke that habit was that occasional and unexpected whack on the back of the head that was followed by the motherly refrain: 'Stop that!'

Mothers everywhere tried to break us out of our habits using one of two rationales. Either the habit was irritating, like breathing through your mouth or forgetting to breathe completely, or it was something that would maim us for life, like thumb sucking, which according to my mother could cause buck teeth. And in some cases, like knuckle cracking – which created that ear-rattling sound and would put our joints out of whack – it was both.

Still, as kids, we could ignore those warnings and continue with our detrimental habits, content in our youthful bliss and ignorance. Who really cared about those ghastly side effects that your mum worried about? What twelve-year-old is concerned about buck teeth or sore hands in old age?

So why did we engage in these silly habits anyway? Some of us did it to annoy our parents. But studies suggest that many of the habits we couldn't live without are innate. They are behaviours we engage in because they make us feel comfortable. In some cases, they are even essential to survival. Take thumb sucking. Children engage in it because it feels good and eventually turns into a mechanism that eases anxiety. But it's also an act that is so instinctive that human babies have been observed on sonograms sucking their thumbs even before they are born. Considering that infants get all their sustenance by nursing, it makes sense. And most people continue some variation of this habit for life. Smoking, nibbling and chewing are all considered extensions of the sucking reflex. No wonder that half of all babies, if left to their own devices, will suck on their thumbs or fingers for hours at a time, whether awake or asleep.

There is even a brain circuit, called the basal ganglia, that is critical to habits, addiction and procedural learning. For a thumb sucker, all it takes is the sight of a thumb to activate this circuit and set in motion the process that leads to the desire to engage in the habit. Same goes for knuckle cracking, and other habits. This brain circuit is hard to rewire, which explains why so many children insist on engaging in bad habits despite warnings from their parents.

But now that we're adults, things are different. All those nasty side effects we were warned about seem much more capable of coming back to haunt us. All of a sudden, arthritis doesn't seem like such a distant threat. The knuckle crackers I know seem to think it's inevitable. So what do we really have to worry about? When was mum fibbing, and when was she telling the truth?

Does cracking your knuckles cause arthritis?

Like the wail of a mobile phone in a theatre or the shriek of fingernails on a blackboard, the sound of knuckles cracking can be a nuisance. It can also have consequences for the person doing the cracking, though urban legend notwithstanding, arthritis isn't one of them.

For ages, parents everywhere have been telling their kids that popping their joints will mess them up in a foolhardy attempt to stop that unsettling, skin-crawling noise. Judging by the number of adults who crack their knuckles so often it appears they're addicted, it's clear that most kids don't exactly have 'arthritis of the hand' near the top of their anxiety lists, right after being picked last for the football team.

Then again, that's not to say this is a myth no one buys. Surveys show that a large percentage of arthritis sufferers attribute their condition at least in part to a lifetime of cracking their knuckles, cracking their toes and just generally doing things with their joints that would make a parent cringe.

But here's what's really going on. The loud 'pop' of a cracked knuckle is caused by synovial fluid, the thick lubricant that surrounds every joint. When you stretch or pull your fingers backward, the bones of the joint pull apart, creating a low-pressure environment that creates a bubble. That bubble does not explode, as most people suspect. It implodes, or collapses in on itself, much like a burned-out star collapsing into a black hole, which sends synovial fluid crashing inward.

Once this big bubble is gone, a smaller one forms in its place. For about ten minutes, it sticks around as the gas is completely absorbed back into the synovial fluid. All that time, tugging on your fingers will cause the small bubble to stretch a bit, but it won't pop – which, by the way, is the reason a single knuckle cannot be cracked more than once in the span of a few minutes.

That noise you hear when the large bubble implodes might be disturbing, but it's not as bad as it sounds. And there are studies that confirm this. One of the largest was published in *Annals of the Rheumatic Diseases* and looked at three hundred healthy people over forty-five years old, about one-fourth of them habitual knuckle crackers.

The rates of arthritis of the hand were similar in both groups, though the knuckle crackers, on average, had reduced grip strength. Knuckle cracking was also associated with higher rates of swelling of the hand, manual labour, smoking and alcohol consumption. A smaller study that appeared in the *Western Journal of Medicine* had similar results.

If you noticed from the previous findings that manual labour was common among the knuckle crackers with reduced grip strength and wondered if that could have played a role in the results, not to worry. Researchers are pretty confident that manual labour cannot be a factor in the findings. If it was, then habitual knuckle crackers would also have higher rates of surgery, trauma and other issues with their hands than those who take their parents' advice and leave their knuckles alone. But they don't.

Case closed. Looks like parents will need a new knuckle-cracking myth to frighten their kids.

Does keeping a wallet in your back pocket cause sciatica?

Although most people consider a fat wallet stuffed with business cards and scraps of paper more of an eyesore than a health hazard, if you carry one of these in your back pocket, you might want to keep the number of a good back specialist in there too, because this one is true.

The phenomenon was first described in an article in the *New England Journal of Medicine* in 1966, just as credit cards, coincidentally, were beginning to proliferate. The report was about a lawyer who suffered aches and pains in his left leg, not far from where he kept a wallet that in the previous three years had been growing thick with charge cards.

'Recently, he learned that removal of the wallet from his left hip pocket brought relief, and reinsertion of the fat wallet reproduced the symptoms,' the report said.

The patient's condition was described as 'credit-carditis'. Unfortunately, that term never quite caught on as a medical diagnosis, but countless reports of similar cases have followed, and doctors say the condition has become increasingly common in the past few decades. Occupation seems to play a major role. People whose jobs are largely sedentary – office workers, truck drivers, taxi drivers, call-centre operators, etc. – are particularly at risk.

The onset of the condition is gradual, caused not only by wallets but by any object that presses on the piriformis muscle in the buttocks, which is connected to the sciatic nerve that runs down the leg. Over time, if you're developing the condition, you'll feel pain radiating down your back and hip area.

'I had to tell one patient with back pain to remove at least twenty years' worth of stored data from his wallet', said Dr Gerard P. Varlotta of the New York University School of Medicine.

Wallets are not the only culprits. According to the medical literature, one man developed the condition from carrying a bunch of handkerchiefs in his back pocket during hay fever season. Another developed it from keeping golf balls in his back pocket on the course.

Fortunately, unlike a lot of other back problems, this one has a very quick and simple remedy. It's referred to by doctors as a 'wallectomy'.

Can drinking coffee stunt a child's growth?

Besides the jitteriness, the insomnia and the prospect of starting every morning in a long line at their local Starbucks, children have, for generations, been given another reason not to drink coffee: it stunts growth. The only problem, it seems, is that after decades of research on the physiological results of coffee consumption, scientists have yet to find any evidence that consuming coffee has an effect on your height.

Those who have studied the claim may well be better off investigating what seems like a far more pressing question: what on earth are kids doing drinking coffee anyway? Do we live in a world of such driven maniacs that even toddlers have to jump-start their days with a cup of liquid energy? Can't they just wake up and have a glass of milk, like the rest of us did when we were kids? One of the studies that investigated the effects of coffee on children included a large group of children in Central America, some of them six-year-olds who were drinking as much as seven ounces of coffee a day. That's nearly a cup.

Parents who insist on letting their kids enjoy a cup of coffee every now and then can at least rest assured that their son isn't killing his chances of hitting six foot three. (And as we learned earlier, tall people, according to scientists, are perceived as smarter, handsomer and nicer, so it's not an idle worry.)

How people started to believe that coffee stunts your growth isn't entirely clear. But scientists believe it has something to do with caffeine, which for many years was thought to be a risk factor for osteoporosis. That concern stemmed from early studies that associated a high intake of caffeinated beverages with reduced bone mass. More recent studies suggest that if there is such an effect, it is both slight and easily offset when dietary intake of calcium is adequate.

There is also another explanation for the association. According to one study by Dr Robert P. Heaney, a calcium expert at Creighton University in Omaha, Nebraska, USA, much of the research linking caffeine consumption to reduced bone mass was conducted on people whose diets were low on milk and other sources of calcium – precisely because they drank so much caffeine-laden coffee and soda instead.

It's not that caffeinated drinks deplete your body of calcium, so much as the fact that, for some people, they end up taking the place of other beverages that *would* give you calcium.

In a related study, scientists tracked eighty-one adolescents for six years and discovered that those who had the highest daily caffeine intake had no difference in bone gain or bone density at the end of the study than those with the lowest. No word though on whether all that caffeine made them more productive at the playground.

Can wearing tight plaits, ponytails or hats make you lose your hair?

It starts with those occasional strands of hair gathering in the drain. After a while, you notice that you can't take a shower without looking down and spying clumps. You start wearing a cap to keep your hair protected from the rough and tumble of daily life. But the clumps just get bigger. What can you do?

Realizing that your hair is slowly disappearing is about as much fun for some people as having a heart attack. In some cases, the one might even lead to the other. But for a lot of us, hair loss is a problem that, like a stroke, can be avoided. While many people don't think twice about laying out huge sums of money for trips to the salon or high-end hair products, rarely do we actually stop to consider that some of our hairstyles can carry additional costs.

Tight ponytails, buns, plaits and other hairstyles – not to mention hats of all types – can pull on your scalp for extended periods of time and cause irreversible hair loss, a condition doctors refer to as traction alopecia. Ever notice how Andre Agassi always wore hats and quickly went bald? Call it a coincidence – but that hat certainly didn't help.

There are no figures on how many people suffer hair loss because of what they do or add to their hair, but the problem is most common in women and children. Years ago, it was a frequent scourge among nurses, who often used pins to secure their caps to their scalps for hours at a time. One study in the

International Journal of Dermatology looked at nurses and found that some had hair loss at the exact site where they used pins to secure their caps.

At the root of traction alopecia is excessive tension on the scalp. The first signs are inflamed follicles, thickened or scaly skin, and, in some cases, small pustules. Over time, you'll notice large amounts of broken strands around your scalp. Your hair, instead of being long and thick, will be short and thin – particularly in spots where you've worn buns, plaits or put tension on your scalp.

Balding occurs if the problem is ignored for long enough. But if detected early, it can be reversed. Or it can be avoided altogether by limiting your use of tight curlers and chemical straighteners and by relaxing any tension on your scalp.

Does crossing your legs cause varicose veins?

More than twelve large studies that have looked at the risk factors for varicose veins have not found leg crossing to be one of them.

That may come as a shock to any woman who recalls the old saying about never crossing your legs at the dinner table. Bad manners? Certainly. But a bad habit? No, despite the consensus that the advice has more to do with concerns about varicose veins than anything else. It's the same reason that nurses have been wearing soft shoes for ages and women who wear tall heels have long been advised to slip off their shoes every hour or two and flex their toes: to relieve pressure in their calves (and their backs).

About half of all women and 15 per cent of men over fifty develop the swollen and unsightly blood vessels that characterize varicose veins, caused by blood pooling in the legs. Women who refuse to part with their stilettos may be increasing their risk, but those who cross their legs are safe.

A study of 3,822 adults, published in 1988, found that for men, the strongest risk factors were smoking and low levels of physical activity. For women, a lack of exercise, high blood pressure and obesity were strongly linked to the condition.

Standing or engaging in sedentary activities for more than eight hours a day increased the risk as well – a finding that has been borne out in European studies of people whose jobs require them to be on their feet, such as nurses. Other studies have pointed to pregnancy and constantly wearing high heels as major contributors.

But perhaps the easiest way to determine your risk is to consult your family tree – more than 80 per cent of people with varicose veins have at least one parent with them.

Does reading in the dark damage your eyes? What about wearing glasses?

Anyone who has ever held a flashlight to a book to read into the small hours of the night has heard the dire warnings about reading in the dark. It will weaken your eyes. It will ruin your vision.

But while reading in the dark might strain your eyes and give you a headache, the notion that it can cause lasting damage is all wrong. Most people can expect to experience some decline in their vision as they age, and genetic research shows that it is family history above all else that determines to what extent your vision will weaken.

Some researchers, however, argue that putting too much strain on your eyes as a child or young adult, like the kind caused by reading in the dark or simply reading for prolonged periods in general, might contribute to the decline of your eyesight later in life.

Population studies have shown that the rates and severity of myopia are always greatest among people who attain the highest levels of education, as well as those whose occupations require them to do a great deal of reading, like lawyers, editors and doctors.

Think about it. How many corporate lawyers do you see wearing glasses? A lot more than the number of lorry drivers, that's for sure.

But a problem with this argument is that most studies that support it do not take into account class and economic differences. Simply put, people with less access to higher education are also going to have less access to eye doctors. So any eye problems they have are more likely to go untreated.

Most ophthalmologists and eye experts, like Dr Robert Cykiert at New York University Medical Centre, USA, are adamant that the strain reading puts on your eyes – in poor light or not – is safe. 'It may create fatigue,' he explained, 'but it can't hurt your eyes in any way.'

You can also put another popular vision myth to bed – that wearing glasses weakens your eyes. Sure, glasses can bring a blurry world into focus. But it's commonly thought that by doing all the heavy lifting, they can also speed the natural decline of vision.

It's yet another optical illusion. How well a person can see is largely determined by the size of the eyeball, something a pair of glasses or reading in the dark cannot change. The average eye is about an inch from the cornea, in the front, to the retina, in the back. When the eyes are either too large (short-sightedness) or too small (far-sightedness), the cornea cannot properly focus images on the retina, and glasses can help compensate.

The contrast between poor and normal vision becomes more obvious when people wear glasses for a while and then take them off. But glasses have no lasting effect on eyesight.

Can hypnosis help you stop smoking?

Mark Twain had a good line about the pains of quitting smoking. 'It's easy,' he said, 'I've done it a thousand times.'

In actuality, though, anyone who has ever tried it knows how tough it can be. Nicotine is one of the most notoriously addictive drugs in the world, right up there with alcohol, opium and cocaine. More than three-quarters of smokers who try to quit end up relapsing several times, no matter what they try to break their habit.

And hypnosis, it seems, is about as effective as many other techniques – and that means not very.

Several studies have confirmed this. In one of the largest, a meta-analysis published in 2000, researchers reviewed five dozen previous studies that looked at hypnosis and smoking cessation. It found that those who tried it had an abstinence rate of 20 to 30 per cent after one year. Not bad, right?

But few people try one cessation technique all by itself. A lot of studies that looked at the success of hypnosis found that it was being used in combination with counselling and other treatments, so it's hard to determine the precise efficacy of that one approach.

For reasons that are not entirely clear, men have slightly higher success rates after hypnosis than women. Women may be less likely to quit smoking because of concerns about gaining weight. Sounds sexist, I know, but that's what scientists who study this stuff seem to think.

The weight gain side effect is no exaggeration (it happens to both men and women). Smoking is horrible for every part of you except your metabolism; it forces your body to expend extra energy trying to detoxify itself from the chemicals being inhaled.

If this metabolic dip is a big concern, try exercising and munching on a combination of Nicorette and Jolt chewing gums. A study in the *American Journal of Clinical Nutrition* found that nicotine gum that also contains caffeine can help offset the metabolic slowdown by creating a 10 per cent increase in your metabolism.

That and a few sessions of hypnosis might not get you to kick your habit right away, but they'll at least get you on the path to a long, smoke-free life.

Are heart attacks more common on Mondays?

Stress. It's a habitual part of modern life, especially the modern work week.

The stress of returning to work and five long days before the next weekend seems reason enough to dread Monday mornings. And it's long been suspected that the stress of that cursed first day of the week might also be a hazard to your heart.

Everyone knows Mondays are a drag. They've been the scariest day of the week since the start of the lunar calendar. The anxiety of getting ready for the week ahead can be so overwhelming that plenty of people sleep fine all week and then toss and turn on Sunday nights, particularly those whose jobs are packed with stress. Then there's the depression that sets in when you realize the weekend has come to a close, the Monday morning headache that hits coffee drinkers who down a cup or two too many to get back into the grind and the jump in blood pressure caused by Monday morning traffic.

Ideally, we would all skip that first day of the week, but without that time-traveller's luxury, we are stuck with the consequences – and there are plenty. In several studies over the years, scientists have found that deaths from heart attacks follow a pattern: they occur at their lowest rates on weekends, jump significantly on Mondays and then drop again on Tuesdays.

One of the largest and most recent studies to examine this trend, published in the *European Journal of Epidemiology*, found that the risk of a heart attack is about 20 per cent greater on Mondays for adult men and 15 per cent greater for adult women.

Why? Our blood pressure soars on Monday mornings, and scientists have devised some unusual studies over the years to prove it. My favourite is a Japanese study that outfitted 175 people to measure their blood pressure twenty-four hours a day, seven days a week. In the name of science, they were forced to lug special blood pressure devices around, something that probably just made their blood pressure even higher. But what the scientists discovered was a surge in blood pressure on Monday mornings that dwarfed the increase on any other day of the week. People who didn't have to work Monday mornings, meanwhile, had no surge in blood pressure that day.

Looking at when in the day heart attacks occur and what can set them off has been a favourite subject of researchers for decades, ever since scientists discovered in the 1980s that people are most likely to suffer heart attacks in the morning, even during the weekend, when they aren't trying to rush to work or school. The simple act of waking up can even be a culprit.

It's easy to blame the stress of returning to work for the increased risk on Monday mornings, and surely that plays a significant part. But other factors may be involved. In the Scottish population the risk is greatest among people who drink heavily over the weekend suggesting that weekend binge drinking might play a role. It's also been shown that the increased risk applies to the retired – people who presumably are no longer worried about overbearing bosses and heavy workloads. Much like a case of post-traumatic stress disorder after a terrifying ordeal, the psychological terror of waking up on Monday morning never seems to leave, even in retirement.

How about on birthdays – are you more likely to have a heart attack then?

If the strain of physical exertion or merely the day of the week can set off a heart attack, then why not the emotions associated with a birthday?

Birthdays are typically considered a time of celebration, a day to gather around a cake with our closest friends and relatives and get all sentimental. But for some, they can also be filled with anguish and pressure, a day of silent despair or of expectations unfulfilled. That, scientists say, is particularly true with the elderly, who are more likely on birthdays to begin to think of their lives in terms of how much time is left, rather than how much time has passed.

One of the largest and most intriguing studies to take a close look at birthdays was published in the journal *Neurology* and involved tracking more than fifty thousand patients, with an average age of about seventy, who were treated for heart failure at hospitals over a two-year period. What the study found was a strong relationship between birthdays and the onset of so-called vascular events.

Strokes, acute myocardial infarctions, and transient ischemic attacks were 27 per cent more likely to occur on birthdays than on other days of the year. Yet there was no corresponding increase for other types of illness, like appendicitis, head trauma or symptoms of asthma, suggesting that heart attacks were unique. Those who study heart attacks and the events that touch them off attributed the phenomenon largely to anxiety and other 'psychosocial stressors', but additional factors appear to be involved.

Another large study in New Jersey in 1993 found a similar birthday peak – 21 per cent for men and 9 per cent for women – suggesting that overindulgence (ah, yes, that favourite habit) plays some sort of role. Drinking and smoking, for instance, are more common on birthdays, particularly among men, a finding that could explain the gender difference in the study. The bottom line: susceptible people may want to avoid salt, alcohol and brisk physical activity on their birthdays.

And definitely make sure no one's planning any big surprise parties – those things can kill you.

Does the stress of the festive season cause an increase in heart attacks and depression?

Despite the notion that the holiday season is filled with joy, we all know that it's also a time that can be fraught with stress, depression, and – for some – loneliness. Then there's the panic of last-minute shopping, the agony of dealing with in-laws and the nuisance of navigating jam-packed airports.

All of this can make the holidays more a season of headaches than celebration. So it is small wonder that medical folklore has forged a stubborn link between the holidays and all sorts of sickness, two in particular: heart attacks and depression.

But for all the talk, studies have uncovered little evidence that holiday stress contributes much to the development of either. When it comes to depression, the rates of diagnosis don't climb significantly around Christmas or New Year's Eve. In fact, studies have found what looks to be the opposite: psychiatric visits tend to dip in the weeks before Christmas and then rise afterwards. One study reviewed a thirty-five-year period and saw virtually no relationship between the holidays and suicides. If anything, it seems, people with depression have fewer problems in December, possibly because they have more family and friends around to help them cope.

One exception is seasonal affective disorder, a form of depression that's closely associated with winter. This condition, which is easily treatable, however, has more to do with the short, dark winter days than with holiday stress.

When it comes to heart attacks, on the other hand, there is evidence of a so-called holiday effect – though it's not what you'd think. Deaths from heart disease dip just before major social occasions, like winter holidays and cultural events, and then jump sharply when the day comes – and the day after.

A study in the journal *Circulation* looked at millions of deaths over the last thirty years and found that the largest rises in deaths from heart disease occurred on Christmas Day, December 26, and New Year's Day. The rate on those days, in fact, was a staggering 11.9 per cent higher than normal for that time of the year. But this effect didn't apply only to heart attacks. It also applied to deaths from natural causes and other diseases, indicating pretty strongly that stress wasn't the primary trigger.

Instead, the risk comes down to two subtle but important factors: staffing and shift changes at hospitals that result in poorer medical care, and patients who delay treatment until the holidays are over.

9
Modern Times
How safe is your mobile phone?

There is no question about it: technology sets the pace today.

We have BlackBerries to tether us to the office, computers to connect us to the whole wide world, microwaves to cook our food in an instant, cars to keep us moving, mobile phones to keep us talking, iPods to keep us humming and televisions to keep us entertained. Everywhere around us, there are gadgets large and small designed to make our lives easier, quicker and more efficient.

And we're all affected. Take a walk around the streets of Britain and you'll be startled to discover that the average person – with all his digital devices – seems like a one-man mobile office. To the extent that living like this allows us to accomplish more with our lives, that can be a good thing.

But it is also inherently human to wonder whether all this technological progress poses some perils. And not just in the Hollywood-inspired, science-fiction sense that one day all these machines will rise up and turn against us. Most of us worry about the more subtle costs of living in a world where – when it comes down to it – almost everything we're exposed to is unnatural. We spend most of our lives in air-conditioned, artificially lit homes and offices that are noisy, dusty and far removed from the plains where our ancestors once roamed.

Technology may have some obvious benefits, but it also forces us to put up with some strange side effects. Our food, for example, is genetically altered. Our phones leak radiation. Our televisions strain our eyes. Our aeroplanes expose us to X-rays. Our microwaves literally irradiate our food. And our indoor plumbing – well, even that's not the straightforward convenience it seems.

What's more, much of modern technology is so relatively new that, in a way, we are all part of an experiment. We almost always obsess over the risks of things before we have had the time to study and fully understand their long-term safety. Mobile phones have only been around long enough for scientists to know the hazards they pose in the short term, say, using one every day for four or five years. But is the risk any greater when a person uses one virtually every day for over a decade, or, as the pre-teens with their crazy ringtones will eventually find out, over the course of a lifetime?

It's natural to wonder how all our artificial devices are affecting our bodies and our health.

Do you risk electrocution if you shower during a thunderstorm? How about talking on the phone?

It sounds too bizarre to be true, but the answers to these questions illustrate that sometimes the medical absurdities we shrug off as myth are not so bogus after all.

When I first heard this warning years ago, I took it as a sign that my parents were losing their marbles. *Get out of the bath because there's thunder outside?* You have got to be joking, I thought. Sure, everyone knows from summers at the swimming pool that water attracts lightning, but your bathroom is a tad

more protected. And if ever there was a good time to take a nice, long, hot, relaxing shower, it's when I'm stuck inside because the weather is nasty. My dad had to be making it up – in all likelihood, he was just wanting me to speed up my luxuriating and save some money on the water bill. So I was eager to see this myth finally crumble under my reportorial scrutiny, like so many that had come before it.

Instead, I found myself eating humble pie.

The basis of the claim that people can be electrocuted in their homes during a thunderstorm is that a bolt of lightning that hits a building – even one that is protected against severe weather – can travel through plumbing, into metal pipes and wiring, and shock anyone who comes into contact with a tap or appliance. Metal pipes are not only excellent conductors of electricity, but they also carry tap water laden with impurities that help conduct electrical current.

Lightning may look spectacular and ferocious, but it's inherently lazy. When a bolt of lightning strikes, the current follows the path of least resistance to the ground, meaning it will gladly jump from a good conductor (a metal pipe) to a much better one (you). If the current from a strike is loosed in your water pipes and you happen to be standing in the bath twisting the hot water tap, your morning shower just might pack a little extra punch.

To be sure, in the real world, the odds of this happening are pretty minute. But it happens, and sometimes with amusing results. In October 2006, a twenty-seven-year-old woman in Croatia was brushing her teeth at home when lightning struck her building and made its way to her tap. As the woman was rinsing her mouth in the sink, the current entered her body and exited – no lie – through her backside.

'I felt it pass through my torso and then I don't remember much at all,' the woman, Natasha Timarovic, was quoted as saying in *The Times* and other news outlets.

Putting aside the crude but irresistible jokes about her 'ring of fire' or 'need to feel the thunder', it turns out that the lightning may have failed to earth through the woman's feet because she was wearing cheap rubber-soled shoes. According to her doctors, those rubber shoes – or, as a scientist might say, 'those poor electrical conductors' – probably saved her life.

Perhaps I should invest in some bathroom flip-flops.

One scientist who can rattle off so many absurd tales like this one that he could easily make a living charging fees as a dinner guest is Ron Holle, a former meteorologist with the US National Oceanic and Atmospheric Administration. Holle, who spends much of his time tracking lightning injuries, estimated that ten to twenty people are shocked every year in the United States alone while bathing, using taps or handling appliances during thunderstorms. Roughly one of those poor souls is actually killed each year.

'There are a ton of myths about lightning,' he told me, 'but this is not one of them.'

In a storm, a protected building acts somewhat like a metal cage. Electricity from a lightning strike is conducted around you and eventually dissipates into the ground. That is why those lightning rods stationed on top of your building are so important: they can safely direct the current to the ground.

There is no real risk other than your plumbing unless you happen to be touching something connected to a conducting path and your building does not have a lightning rod or is not properly grounded. Nowadays, in urban settings at least, most buildings and utilities are well grounded. Freak accidents do occur, but they're rare.

Mary Ann Cooper, a doctor who runs the Lightning Injury Research Programme at the University of Illinois at Chicago, said people have been shocked and even killed while chatting on the phone during thunderstorms – another long-standing fear. In 1985, for example, a student in New Jersey, USA was killed when a bolt of lightning caused an electrical surge to flow through his telephone wire, enter his ear and stop his heart. Investigators later found that the telephone lines in his home were not grounded because the wiring had not been installed properly.

And you thought *your* phone company was bad.

Can watching too much television shorten a child's attention span?

We truly live in the age of TV. And we're not just TV lovers, we're TV junkies. The average child watches about four hours of television a day and each year sees thousands of films, shows and television advertisements. By the time the average teenager leaves school, they have spent half as much time sitting in a classroom as they have sitting on a sofa with their eyes glued to the television.

Considering all the quality time that kids are spending with their television sets these days, it's worth addressing that age-old question: are televisions turning children into morons?

There's no doubt that watching television is strongly associated with low intelligence. Plenty of studies show that children who watch a dozen or more hours of television each week have lower reading scores and generally do less well academically than their peers whose parents have no problem flicking the 'off' switch. But that doesn't prove that television directly harms the brain; it can also be argued that watching it simply deprives you of study time.

So to answer the question more directly, scientists have been trying to find a link between watching television and decreased attention span, particularly in infants and toddlers. That's because in the first few years of life, the brain develops swiftly. It's commonly thought that stimulating environments – like the rapid-fire stimulation of television – can set off changes in the brain.

But permanent damage?

Apparently, yes. A study of 2,500 children published in the American journal *Pediatrics* found that the more television children between the ages of one and three watch, the greater their risk of having attention deficit hyperactivity disorder (ADHD) at age seven. In some cases, all it took was an extra hour of television a day to heighten the odds of developing the disorder by a staggering 10 per cent. And previous studies of television and its link to ADHD had similar findings.

But parents who cringe at the sound of that can breathe a little easier. Two other large, careful studies that followed failed to find any link between television exposure and symptoms of

ADHD at all, including one study that looked at five thousand kindergarteners across the country. What most scientists suspect is that there is some small effect, but that it's probably minor. In a country such as America where half of all households have three or more televisions and nearly 60 per cent of children have a television in their bedroom, let's hope they're right.

But even then, there remain concerns. Too much television has been linked to poor sleep, a greater likelihood of taking up smoking, and obesity. It takes about five or more hours of TV viewing a day to see such effects in your life.

Does sitting too close to the TV damage your eyes?

It was more than seventy years ago that television sets first went on sale, and something tells me it was just as long ago that a cautious mother, noticing a son or daughter propped in front of that mesmerizing new invention, snapped and barked the words that children have grown up hearing ever since: 'Get away from the screen; you'll ruin your eyes!'

One small difference between then and now? Today, scientists can say with certainty that the warning is a sham.

Before the 1950s, television sets emitted levels of radiation that after repeated and extended exposure could have heightened the risk of eye problems in some people. Several studies that were conducted before 1970 showed that the levels of radiation emitted by televisions were precariously high. Some even gave off X-rays. A small percentage were above the recommended cut-off of about 0.5 millirems per hour.

But modern televisions are a far different machine. Not only are they made with better shielding, they also use lower voltage, so radiation is no longer an issue. According to some studies, the average dose of radiation experienced by a person who watches television regularly and sits within a few feet of their television set is about 1 millirem over the course of a year – about a tenth of the amount of radiation you'd get from a single chest X-ray.

'This is not an old wives' tale; it's an old technology tale,' observed Dr Norman Saffra, the chairman of ophthalmology at Maimonides Medical Centre in Brooklyn, New York. 'Based on the world our grandmothers lived and grew up in, it was an appropriate recommendation.'

But those days are gone. Feel free to sit as close to the television as you want – whether it's to get a better look at those gorgeous doctors on *ER*, or to test the theory that if you sit close enough, you'll be transported inside.

Keep in mind, though, that while concentrating on a screen for hours on end may not cause blindness, it can lead to eye strain. Keeping the room fairly well lit while the television is on and peeling your eyes from the screen every now and then can help prevent this.

Parents should also be alert for the child who keeps creeping closer to the screen. Not because of radiation, of course, but because it's a sign that your child may need glasses.

Can loud music cause permanent hearing loss?

The amplified din of a rock concert or a few hours at a noisy bar can numb your ears for a day or two. But will it make you go deaf?

Studies show that most people regularly experience levels of noise and music that, over time, can leave them hard of hearing for life. No surprise, then, that a third of all cases of permanent hearing loss are caused by noise from recreational and work-related activities.

In most cases, the damage is often accompanied by a non-stop buzzing called tinnitus, which is a lot worse than it sounds. Imagine a fly circling your ear that, no matter how many times you swat at it, just won't go away – for life.

There are two types of noise that can cause this type of hearing loss: loud impulse noise, like an explosion, or loud continuous noise, like the kind that pours through your window at 6 a.m. when a construction crew decides to repave the street in front of your house for the next eight months. Both types can harm extremely sensitive hair cells in the inner ear as well as the hearing nerve.

All it takes to get to this point are repeated doses of noise at levels between 90 decibels and 140 decibels. Those levels are fairly common. The clamour at most bars and clubs registers 110 to 120 decibels. Amplified music at a concert can reach 120 decibels and climb to an ear-throbbing 130 decibels, rivalling the sound of a jet taking off. Heavy traffic can reach 85 decibels.

But the most pervasive – and yet widely unknown – threat to our eardrums are those sleek MP3 players we all carry around these days. The sound they produce can soar to 100 decibels – louder than a lawnmower.

While most people covet the hours of non-stop music and the small, snug earpieces that come with their MP3 players, those are also the features that make them such a hazard to your ears.

In a study published in 2004 in the journal *Ear and Hearing*, Dr Brian Fligor of Harvard Medical School looked at a variety of headphones and found that the smaller they were, the higher their output levels at any given volume control setting.

Compared with larger headphones that cover the entire ear, some insertable headphones, like the white ones sold with iPods, increased sound levels by up to 9 decibels. That may not seem like much, but because decibels are measured in logarithmic units, it can mean the difference between the noise output of an alarm clock and a chainsaw.

The other problem is that the insertable headphones that come with MP3 players are not as efficient at blocking background noise as the larger ones that cover the ear, so there is more incentive to turn up the volume, and many of us do just that.

Can you hear me now?

Does too much noise increase your risk of a heart attack?

Researchers have long suspected that too much exposure to everyday noise – sirens, chaos at the office – can increase blood pressure and take a toll on your health. You know that irritation you feel every time a rubbish van rumbles past your house or the sound of a road drill hits your ears? Well, think of what all that frustration can do over the course of a lifetime.

The physiological chain reaction that occurs when you're jarred by a loud and oppressive noise goes something like this: the noise causes a psychological reaction first – anger, stress or fear, for instance – which then causes levels of adrenalin and other sweat-inducing hormones to soar. Ultimately, that increases your blood pressure, your plasma lipid levels and, crucially, your risk of cardiovascular disease.

Like all things in life, women and men seem to react differently when it comes to the toll of loud noises on their bodies, and it also varies enormously from one person to the next. No one is completely sure why. Genetics and personality certainly play a role, and it may have something to do with ingrained evolutionary differences in the way men and women generally cope with emotional hardships. Men, for example, are more likely to suffer heart attacks when stressed because they release hormones such as testosterone, which amplifies that dangerous chain reaction of increasing blood pressure and plasma lipid levels. Women, on the other hand, tend to respond to stress by releasing hormones like oxytocin, which has a calming, soothing effect.

On a more basic scientific level, a few studies over the years have found that there is indeed a link between constant exposure to noise of all kinds and a higher risk of heart disease.

One of the more interesting studies was published in the *European Heart Journal*. It looked at the levels of work and environmental noise that four thousand people – half of them heart attack survivors – were experiencing daily and found that chronic noise exposure, after adjusting for factors like smoking and age, was responsible for a 'mild to moderate' increase in the risk of heart disease. (Other studies have gone further and found that people who wear earplugs at work have a lower risk than their colleagues who don't.)

When it came to the rumble and commotion of traffic and other environmental noises, women showed nearly a threefold increase in their risk and men nearly a 50 per cent increase. Women, though, didn't seem to be affected by high levels of noise in the office, even though for men it increased the risk by nearly a third.

It's not clear why, but some scientists think women may have an easier time adjusting to the types of noise that are more common in the office setting: talking, chit-chat and the occasional verbal spat. Then again, there's no real way to confirm that this is the case. It's technically a hypothesis, which amounts to the scientific equivalent of an assumption. Translation: your guess is as good as mine.

Do microwave ovens kill the nutrients in your food?

They're a staple in kitchens and eating establishments everywhere, but people still suspect that the radiation put out by microwave ovens can ruin the healthfulness of their food, destroying all sorts of vitamins and nutrients.

Chalk it up to our good old mistrust of anything that brings to mind radiation. We associate power lines with cancer, mobile phones with brain tumours and nuclear reactors with grave danger. So of course it follows that microwaves would be given the same treatment. I've even been asked by some people whether just standing in front of a microwave is enough to give you cancer (um, no).

And all over the Internet, there are anti-microwave rants and diatribes. They all say the same thing: microwaves suck the vitamins right out of your food. One popular website says that eating food cooked à la microwave will raise your cholesterol, cause a drop in haemoglobin, 'destabilize' your cells – essentially everything but cause you to grow horns.

That sounds like a bit much considering that microwaves warm up food by causing the molecules in it to vibrate, basically an accelerated version of what happens in the oven. And a quick look at the science shows that microwaves have little or no effect on nutritional value.

To be sure, every cooking method can destroy vitamins and other nutrients in food. The factors that determine the extent of the damage are how long the food is cooked, how much liquid is used and the cooking temperature. Since microwave ovens often use less heat than conventional methods and involve shorter cooking times, they generally have the least destructive effects.

The most heat-sensitive nutrients are water-soluble vitamins, like folic acid and vitamins B and C, which are common in vegetables.

In studies at Cornell University, scientists looked at the effects of cooking on water-soluble vitamins in vegetables and found that spinach retained nearly all of its folate when cooked in a microwave, but lost about 77 per cent when cooked on a hob. They also found, surprisingly, that bacon cooked by microwave has significantly lower levels of cancer-causing nitrosamines than conventionally cooked bacon.

When it comes to vegetables, cooking them by microwave is only problematic if you add water, which greatly accelerates the loss of nutrients. A 2003 study in the *Journal of the Science of Food and Agriculture* found that broccoli cooked by microwave – and immersed in water – loses about 74 per cent to 97 per cent of its antioxidants. When steamed or cooked without water, the broccoli retains most of its nutrients.

Can flying increase the risk of a miscarriage?

Hopping on a plane and flying for hours at a time is generally considered more of a nuisance than a health concern. But when it comes to a woman who is travelling for two, are the stakes a little higher?

Scientists have speculated for decades that frequent flying can heighten the risk of complications during pregnancy, arguing that low levels of oxygen, increased exposure to radiation and other conditions aboard aircraft can harm a developing foetus. Some suspect it can even cause birth defects. (For every three or four hours of flight, you're exposed to the radiation equivalent of a chest X-ray.)

In centuries past, this would never have been an issue. For safety reasons, the nine months of pregnancy used to be known widely as a woman's 'time of confinement', a time when a pregnant woman quit work, stayed at home and cut off all social ties. Back then, allowing an expectant mother to take long trips by horse and cart (much less by air!) would have been unheard of.

Today, of course, that would never happen. Having a baby for many women simply means factoring morning sickness, some extra trips to the doctor and a couple of weeks of maternity leave into an already busy schedule. Surveys show that while many pregnant women fear the potential effects of flying on their babies, many feel they have no choice but to continue flying if it means risking their careers to abstain.

Fortunately, women who rack up their frequent flyer miles while pregnant can do so without regret. A handful of studies have looked closely at air travel and the risk of complications and so far none have uncovered any solid link. One of the more extensive studies was published in 1999 and focused on women who fly more than anyone: flight attendants.

From 1973 to 1994, the study, published in the *Journal of Occupational and Environmental Medicine*, examined the medical records and work activity of 1,751 pregnant flight attendants. Although it did not find high rates of complications, it did find that the flight attendants who worked during the early stages of pregnancy had a slightly higher risk of miscarriage than their peers who took time off.

But it was unclear whether undue stress or various other factors were to blame. Another study published a year earlier, for example, showed that while pregnant flight attendants who logged a lot of hours had a higher risk of miscarriage than their colleagues who took time off, they had the same risk of miscarriage as other working women (about 10 to 20 per cent).

After reviewing years of research, the American College of

Obstetricians and Gynaecologists released a report in 2001 saying that radiation exposure for the typical pregnant air traveller was minimal, and that the low pressures in the cabin were unlikely to affect oxygen supply to a foetus. The group recommended that women fly only up until their thirty-sixth week of pregnancy – not because there is any risk to the baby after that, but because you risk going into labour during a flight.

Is the back of an aeroplane the safest place to sit?

OK. So you have to put up with the engine noise, the bathroom traffic, and, of course, the ugly prospect of being the last person off the plane. But I've always been told that flying economy class is a blessing in disguise.

Irritating as it may be, sitting in the back of a plane is supposedly a good way to lower your odds of getting hurt in a crash. Put aside for a second the fact that the odds of surviving a major crash are miniscule no matter where you sit. Some people argue that, theoretically, the rear section of a plane is safer than the front because aeroplanes always seem to crash nose first (have you ever seen a plane hit the ground at top speed tail first?). Others argue that the wing portion is the safest section, saying that it makes sense from an engineering standpoint, since the wing is more structurally stable.

Or maybe it's something else. Maybe those of us who find ourselves relegated to economy class need the consolation of an urban legend to get us past those cold, snooty, privileged stares in first class. I know I sometimes do. ('Enjoy that extra leg room and your glass of Merlot, mate. If this plane goes down, you're out of luck.')

But whatever the reason, the notion that one section of a plane is any safer than another is not supported by the facts. Take it from Todd Curtis, PhD, an aviation safety expert who literally wrote the book on aviation safety data, called *Understanding Aviation Safety Data*. Brainy and bespectacled, Curtis keeps a detailed, no-nonsense, almost disturbing database of airline accidents and crashes at airsafe.com that can answer all sorts of grim (and not so grim) questions about flying.

But sometimes there is no simple yes or no answer. Poring over the details of countless airline mishaps going back decades, it's easy to see that every crash is so unique, with so many variables – did the plane break apart? Did it catch fire? Did it collide in mid-air? Did it go down over water? – that it's impossible to say that one seat is always safer than another.

The other problem is that most countries do not have agencies that conduct thorough accident investigations after every crash. And even with detailed information, like seating maps, it is difficult to determine where people were sitting or standing at the precise time of impact.

There are plenty of accidents in which only passengers in the front of the plane survived, like the one in which a commuter plane crashed in Kentucky in August 2006, killing every person aboard but a single co-pilot in the cockpit. And conversely, there are plenty of crashes where only people in the rear survived. A good example is the 737 that crashed head first into the Potomac River in Washington, D.C., in 1982, killing seventy-four of the seventy-nine people aboard. The survivors only made it because the back of the plane was the only part that stayed above water for a few minutes after impact.

'If I knew a plane was crashing, the safest seat would be outside of the airplane,' Curtis told me, only half jokingly. 'Because the only way I can tell you which seat is technically the safest is to know what kind of crash dynamics we're looking at.'

So what can you do to improve your odds? Most accidents occur while planes are descending, approaching the runway, or landing (about 60 per cent) or during the take-off and climbing phases (35 per cent), so Curtis said it's best to fly non-stop, which reduces your exposure to these accident-prone stages of flight. A single, non-stop flight is safer than multiple short flights, even if that flight is six hours long.

As a rule, larger planes are safer than smaller ones, partly because they are subject to stricter safety regulations, but also because they have more structure that can absorb energy during an impact. Smaller aircraft have a larger percentage of crashes with 100 per cent fatality rates than larger planes (ones that can carry more than thirty passengers).

What that means is if you're ever on an aeroplane that's going down, pray it's a 737 and not a Cessna.

Do mobile phones really cause brain cancer?

If you're like most people, you've wondered whether the hours and hours (and hours and hours) you've spent talking on your mobile phone will come back to haunt you. Or maybe you're one of the four or five holdouts who still hasn't got a mobile phone. In that case, you might not be completely opposed to all those loudmouths you've put up with over the years getting a good dose of karma.

Mobile phones throw off a type of low energy radiation known as radiofrequency energy, and nothing in this world is more closely associated with cancer risk than exposure to radiation. Then there's this: at the same time that mobile phones began popping up around this country like ants at a picnic, there also seemed to be a slight increase in the rates of brain cancer.

So what gives? In reality, the type of radiation emitted by mobile phones is far different and less harmful than the powerful ionizing radiation you're exposed to through more traditional sources, like medical X-rays. Mobile-phone radiation is similar to the energy microwave ovens use to cook food (and which are considered safe), and it's released in smaller amounts and for longer periods of time.

So the basic question is whether minute levels of radiation, focused on your head for long periods of time, can do any damage.

There are plenty of people who insist that it can. David Reynard, a businessman who worked in the telecommunications industry for years pioneering mobile phones, was one of the first people to file a lawsuit against the mobile-phone industry, alleging in the early 1990s that his wife developed a brain tumour from constantly talking on her mobile phone. Then a few years later, Chris Newman, a doctor – and a neurologist no less – diagnosed the cause of his own brain cancer. In an $800 million lawsuit filed against Motorola, he argued that a brain tumour developed in the exact anatomical spot where radiation from his mobile phone would have permeated his skull.

It's important to note that both of those lawsuits were eventually dismissed for lack of evidence. It's increasingly looking as though the larger scare they helped ignite will meet a similar fate, because scientific data suggests there's not much to it.

There are two different lines of evidence: epidemiological studies on humans and more direct studies on animals. In the lab, scientists have found that animals exposed to radio-frequencies greater than 2,000 megahertz had damaged strands of DNA, resulting in cancerous mutations. But most mobile phones operate in a frequency that is far lower than that; generally the range is between 800 and 1,900 megahertz (and usually on the lower end of the spectrum).

And while a few epidemiological studies have found a link between mobile-phone use and cancer, many more have not.

In 2000, a study by the US National Cancer Institute looked at nearly eight hundred patients with brain tumours and found that they were no more likely to have used mobile phones than a group of healthy subjects. Those who used their phones the most did not have higher rates of cancer, and tumours were no more likely to develop on the side of the head where the device was held than on the other. Another large study published the same year in the *New England Journal of Medicine* had similar results, as did a later study of thousands of mobile-phone users in Denmark. And yet another study in 2006 that found no link, after comparing hundreds of people who had brain tumours to nearly a thousand who didn't, went a step further. It pored over phone company records to make sure subjects' reports of how often they used their phones – and for how long – were accurate.

The US Food and Drug Administration, which regulates radiation emissions from certain electronic devices, has said that there is no scientific evidence linking wireless phones to health problems. Other agencies that have reviewed the evidence have issued similar statements. Seems the most dangerous thing you can do with your mobile phone these days is talk on it while you're driving.

But because mobile phones are relatively new, most studies have looked at phone use only over a period of a few years, not decades. One reason this debate is still alive is that it's technically too early to rule out any longer-term safety risks.

But if chatting on your phone makes you nervous, you can do a few things to limit your risk:

- Get rid of it. This will put a serious cramp on your social life, but think of what you can do with the extra thirty pounds a month you save on phone bills.

- Use a headset or earpiece, so the phone is away from your head.

- Avoid using the phone when it's roaming or the signal strength is low. It's more expensive, certainly. But this also means that the phone is working harder to establish a connection, and thus is emitting more radiation.

- If your phone has an antenna, extend it as far as possible: most of the radiation is focused near the midpoint of the antenna.

10
The Great Outdoors
Sharks and bears and blizzards,
oh my

Say it's a balmy summer day and you're off to the great outdoors. You have plans to hike, camp, fish, ride your mountain bike over some rough terrain, maybe just lay by the beach and take a dip now and then. You've got your first-aid kit, your hiking boots, a Swiss Army knife and a good map. If you're a city boy like me, you've also got at least a gallon of bug spray, a mobile phone, a digital camera and enough trail mix to get you through a week – in case you get stranded.

You think you're prepared, but most likely you're not.

At times, even the most experienced outdoorsmen get injured or face some other obstacle thrown in their way and have no idea what to do. Most studies show in fact that something on the order of 80 per cent of people who participate in outdoor activities – everything from horseback riding along trails to camping – suffer some sort of mishap on a frequent basis while engaged in their activity. Most end up making a mistake that only worsens their predicament, and often it's because they followed some well-known rule or offhand remark about what to do in an emergency – and the advice turned out to be wrong.

I am definitely someone who would fall into that group. Growing up in the city, my ideas of wild animals were pigeons and stray cats. So when the time came actually to experience the great outdoors, my knowledge of what to do in an emergency boiled down to things I picked up from medical myths that should have been quashed a long time ago.

When I was a ten-year-old in summer camp and a friend was bitten by a snake, the first thing that jumped to mind was to suck out the poison and find a tourniquet. When I was stung by a bee, I would always grab a credit card and gently scrape away the stinger, making sure not to squeeze it and inadvertently release more venom. And when a university friend who lives in the countryside visited me a few years ago and discovered that a tick had crawled up his leg and set up camp in his crotch, I scrambled to find a needle and a lighter. (OK, so first I laughed hysterically for a minute. Then I scrambled.)

But most of all, when I think of all the time I squandered sitting by the side of the pool, staring at my watch and hoping an hour would go by so my cheese sandwich could digest and I could *finally* hop in the water . . .

Here, then, is an attempt to rectify all the things we were taught about the great outdoors that are questionable, incomplete or just plain wrong. You never know, some of this stuff might come in handy someday.

Do mosquitoes really attack some people more than others?

They're the unwanted guests that return every summer. They show up in droves, descending on our ankles and arms to feast and provoke fits of swatting and spraying that can leave you out of breath – that is, if you happen to be one of the unlucky ones (and I'm not talking about the castaways on *Lost*). Mosquitoes will attack anything with a pulse; that much we know. But sit out in the grass with a group of people at the height of summer and it's clear that some in the crowd are more likely to be a target than others.

I consider myself one of the unlucky. I can sit in a room with a dozen people and if a mosquito is in our midst, it is guaranteed to home in on me. Even worse, as I'm attacked relentlessly, others right next to me almost always remain bite-free. It's maddening.

So why do these nasty bloodsuckers find some of us so sweet and ignore everyone else? It turns out that we all have the odours and chemicals that mosquitoes find attractive. Some of us are just better at disguising it than others.

Female mosquitoes – the only ones that bite – are attracted to the carbon dioxide that we exhale, our body heat and chemicals in sweat like lactic acid. Obviously, every human has these things in common, as do our warm-blooded animal buddies. But scientists have found that bite-resistant people produce about a dozen compounds that either prevent mosquitoes from detecting them or drive them away. People like me, who get bitten frequently, lack these compounds that can mask their smell.

British scientists first discovered this years ago after doing research on cattle. While observing different herds, they noticed that the number of pests that showed up depended on the presence of certain cows. When these cows were moved to another herd, the pests followed. The researchers eventually found that these individual cows were emitting distinct smells. They later confirmed the same phenomenon in humans.

Why some people and animals have this built-in shield is not yet known. It may have had some crucial evolutionary purpose, like protecting us from malaria and other mosquito-transmitted diseases.

But if you don't have the shield, don't despair. You can make yourself less attractive by using unscented deodorants, moisturizers and soaps. Repellents made with the insect repellent Deet can also make a difference. A study in the *New England Journal of Medicine* in 2002 found that sprays with even small amounts of Deet protected wearers for up to five hours, while special wristbands and sprays made with citronella lasted only minutes.

You might also have heard the old wives' tale about warding off mosquitoes by eating garlic, bananas and other foods. Don't believe it. There is no evidence to back any of this up. You're better off training yourself to become a master swatter, like I have. Or just quietly dab a little honey on the person sitting next to you. Pretty soon, they'll know what the wrath of a bloodthirsty mosquito is like.

Do chiggers burrow under your skin and die there?

The bites start out as small red bumps on a person's arm or leg. Before long, they turn into a cluster of welts that can make a bee sting seem like a pinprick. The pain is so unsettling and lasts for so long that many victims believe the offending pests simply burrowed under their skin and died there.

But what most people think they know about chiggers is wrong.

Myths about the tiny red bugs stem from their resemblance to pests with similar names, like the oddly named jigger flea, which actually does bore through skin. They are also so microscopic, smaller than the full stop at the end of this sentence, that their victims never see them.

Like most bugs, chiggers can penetrate only thin skin, which is why they tend to attack the knees, ankles and hips. They do not feed on blood; instead, they use powerful enzymes to dissolve a person's cells and form a sort of feeding tube, or stylostome, that's used to suck up liquid tissue.

It is this human straw that stays embedded for weeks and causes so much agony, even long after the bug has fallen off.

Taking a warm bath after spending time in grassy areas is usually a good way to prevent chiggers from attaching. But once the first bumps appear, almost nothing can treat them or bring relief other than dabs of lotion or local anaesthetic. It also helps if you curl up in a ball on your sofa and cry in agony while your friends stare at you and laugh – or so I've been told.

Can you remove a tick by burning it?

Ever noticed a tiny speck on your arm and then discovered that what you thought was a piece of dirt was actually a tick? For most people, that moment is about the only time exposing your arm or leg to an open flame can seem like a good idea.

Boy Scout lore and first-aid survival texts are replete with all sorts of bizarre ways to remove a tick, from soaking the repulsive bug in soapy water to smothering it in Vaseline and taking a hot needle to its behind. When my friend discovered that tick embedded in his crotch, he went through every one of the aforementioned techniques, one after another, howling in disbelief. He shook with panic; I shook with laughter; the tick didn't shake at all.

Although conventional wisdom suggests that roasting a tick is the most effective removal method, studies show that it can actually be the worst. That's because while burning the tick into submission may help get it out sooner, it'll also worsen your prognosis.

Getting the tick out as quickly as possible is crucial because the likelihood of your contracting Lyme disease or another infection rises steeply after twenty-four hours. But traumatizing the insect with heat or too much force also carries the risk of making it regurgitate, increasing the chances of it transmitting a pathogen and increasing your likelihood of infection.

In 1996, a team of Spanish researchers reported that in their study of dozens of people who went to a hospital for treatment after trying to extract a tick, they found that those who did so by squeezing, crushing or burning the creatures were far more likely to develop symptoms of Lyme disease and other complications than those who used the proper removal method: grasping the pest as close to your skin as possible with tweezers and gently pulling it straight up. After that, you should pull any remaining pieces out and clean the site with a disinfectant.

Don't expect smothering the louse with Vaseline or nail polish to work either: it can be hours before it dies from suffocation. Other methods that don't work: pulling, twisting or punching the embedded tick or covering it in gasoline. Yes, people have actually tried these things. And no, none of them seem to work.

As for my friend, none of the techniques he tried had any success. Only a doctor's scalpel was able to dislodge the tick, which had apparently been embedded for more than a day. My friend did not get an infection, but he did suffer the embarrassment of having a doctor guffaw when he first realized where the tick had chosen to set up house. For him, it was a medical first.

Should you treat a bee sting by scraping out the stingers?

What could be worse on a perfect summer day, in the middle of a picnic with friends and family, than a sudden, deep, painful bee sting?

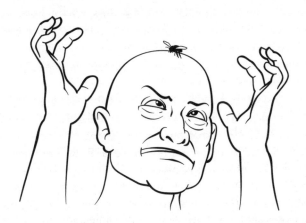

Anyone who has ever felt that dreaded jab knows the shock it brings. As a child, there was nothing I feared more, especially since I always seemed to be as much of a magnet for bees as I am for mosquitoes. On most occasions, the sting would occur in the middle of playing sports. And that was all it took to end my day.

But after every sting, the advice was always the same: find a sharp-edged object, apply it firmly to the skin, and gently scrape away the stinger. I wanted to grab that barbed weapon embedded in my skin and just yank it out, but I was always told not to. This time-honoured advice never to pinch, pluck or grab has been quoted faithfully in medical texts and first-aid guides for generations.

It always seemed logical enough. Since a venom sac is still attached to the rear tip of the stinger, it would seem that pinching or squeezing the barb would be like squeezing a dropper. Doing so would squirt more venom into the wound, making it worse and causing more pain.

That's the conventional thinking and that's what I always grew up believing. But as a health reporter, I discovered that scientists who are familiar with the honeybee anatomy have questioned that wisdom in recent years. The dropper analogy doesn't make as much sense when you consider the way a stinger works. Once you do, you realize that it's speed not style that matters the most when treating a sting.

The crucial detail is that bees leave their victims with more than just a stinger and a venom sac. They also leave behind large parts of their abdomens, which contain clusters of nerves and muscles that vigorously pump more venom into the wound – almost like a valve and piston – even though the bee is long gone. I never stopped to look carefully, and I'm sure no one else does either, but in the first ten to twenty seconds after the eviscerated bee retreats, the barb can be seen visibly twitching, forcing its way deeper into the flesh and depositing more venom.

A study in the *Journal of Allergy and Clinical Immunology* demonstrated this by provoking honeybees into stinging disks made from filter paper and then weighing the papers at different intervals in the stinging process. What they found was that the average stinger, if left in a wound untouched, releases 90 per cent of its venom within twenty seconds. That's a very narrow window of time.

But then another, more courageous team of entomologists set out to document exactly what happens with different methods of removal – using themselves as guinea pigs. In a study published in *The Lancet*, this intrepid and slightly sadistic team had one colleague undergo a series of injections of bee venom to test whether the size of the resulting welt depended on the amount of venom deposited in the skin.

Never mind that the answer is one that, even by the rigorous standards of modern-day science, could have been reached and accepted as fact by logic alone. The pain and size of the welts, of course, increased with the amount of venom used.

After that, the team chose a volunteer for a *second* experiment, this time intended to see whether the amount of time it took to remove a stinger affects the size of the welt. They did this by having the volunteer stand by a hive in a laboratory, catch a worker bee, and press it against a part of his body until it stung. Then the volunteer would scrape away the various stings at various intervals, and on other occasions he would grab and yank it. This crazy experiment involved one volunteer being stung more than fifty times.

But sure enough, timing made all the difference. The longer the stinger stayed in, the bigger the resulting weal – whether it was pinched, squeezed, plucked or scraped. The bottom line: don't stop to think about how you should carefully get a bee stinger out. React instantaneously.

Maybe if I had done that instead of fumbling around for something flat to use to scrape out the stinger, my pain would have been less and my summer days happier.

Should you treat a snakebite by sucking out the venom?

Anyone can tell you how to treat a snakebite in the middle of the woods. Apply a tourniquet, cut the skin, suck out the poison, spit it out and remember to be more careful in the future.

First off, putting your mouth on a venomous wound is the last thing you should do. A study in the *New England Journal of Medicine* in 2002 actually found that cutting, sucking or trying to cut off the blood supply to a bite does more harm than good because it damages nerves, injures blood vessels and heightens your risk of developing a serious infection.

It also delays prompt medical care. What a poisonous bite requires is antivenin and emergency treatment so the best course is to get the injured person to a medical facility as soon as possible. Usually, that's not a problem. Very few people actually die from snakebites and those that do die six to eight hours after the attack, so you actually have plenty of time to get to a hospital.

That last part can't be emphasized enough.

Take it from Dr Barry S. Gold, an assistant professor of medicine at the Johns Hopkins University, Baltimore, Maryland, and a consultant to zoos and poison centres on snakebites. In his decades of dealing with poisonous bites, Gold explained with slight amusement, he has seen a lot of people do some stupid things after being attacked by snakes. People have used stun guns, electrical wire and car batteries on themselves to try to deactivate the venom in their bites. One idiot hooked himself up to the coils of a boat engine, thinking a good strong jolt would do the trick.

Needless to say, when this last idiot came to, the snakebite was the least of his injuries.

'The only thing that's effective is going to the hospital,' Gold insisted.

If you're attacked and bitten, you'll experience nausea, weakness and other symptoms within thirty minutes. In that case, you should do what you can to stay warm and keep the wounded body part below the level of your heart. Try not to run or do anything that can increase your heart rate, because that enhances the absorption of the venom into your bloodstream. Just get to a hospital as fast as possible, in less than a few hours, which shouldn't be a problem unless you live in Siberia. If that's the case, then you can use a tourniquet, but don't try to suck out the venom.

Is it true you should play dead if you're attacked by a bear?

A few years ago, I spent a summer biking with a group of friends. About halfway into our trip, a friend reminded me that if I came dangerously close to a bear while riding my bike, I should throw myself to the ground, curl up in a ball and play dead.

Put aside for a second the fact that if I ever came face to face with a bear in the wild I'd be so immobilized with fear I'd probably lose my ability to think, not to mention control of a range of other bodily functions. What good is playing dead supposed to do? If the bear is wandering around in search of food, doesn't that make his job easier, and me a dead fool?

I couldn't see myself accepting such a fate lying down – literally – so after the trip, when I got home, I riffled through the scientific literature. I was surprised to learn that the strategy of playing dead in the face of an impending attack is not exclusive to humans. Scientists call it extreme immobility and studies show that the line-up of animals that play possum ranges from the Virginia opossum, of course, to bison, ducks, rabbits and snakes.

Animals, like humans, play dead under the assumption that a predator will either lose interest or shift out of attack mode and make a crucial mistake that allows a chance for a clean escape. One study in the 1970s looked at what happened when captive foxes were given a chance to go after live ducks. In every case, the ducks would go limp when the foxes caught them. Sometimes, this worked to their advantage. The foxes would carry them to a storage site and turn their backs, giving the sly ducks an opportunity to get away.

But it worked only a fraction of the time. Most of the time, it simply made the task for the predator easier. Similarly, it's not always such a good idea to play dead with bears, especially since different types of bears attack for different reasons and react in different ways.

Bear attacks can generally be divided into two groups: predatory and defensive. Each calls for a different strategy. Black and grizzly bears, the two you're most likely to confront in the wild, are capable of both types of attack.

Those involving grizzlies tend to be defensive, when the animal feels threatened. Playing dead while lying on your stomach and covering your head and neck lets the bear know you're not a threat and can cause it to back off.

Black bears, on the other hand, are smaller and shyer than grizzlies and usually flee from humans. But when they do attack their motive tends to be predatory, meaning playing dead isn't going to work. Neither will running away. Uphill, downhill or on flatland, it doesn't matter – any bear can outrun even the fastest human. Plus running just makes you look more like prey.

If it looks like the bear is after your food, it's best to drop it and back away. But if it keeps pressing, be aggressive. Yell, shout, bang on objects or use pepper spray. Stand up and raise your arms above your head. Make yourself look as big as possible to scare it off. Most wildlife organizations agree that different circumstances call for different measures. It's not always best to make yourself look like an easy meal.

Can you fight off a shark by punching it in the nose? And was it your brightly coloured swimming costume that caught its eye?

Forget for a moment that the odds of being attacked by a shark at the beach are minuscule. Now imagine a dip in the ocean this summer turning into a tense encounter with a great white, its massive head within arm's reach and powerful jaws closing in.

If you spend enough time watching the Discovery channel, you might hear that the thing to do is to slug it in the snout. This, according to television shows, is a shark's most sensitive area, so it makes sense to zero in on it.

That is, unless you plan on getting away. Despite the common belief that the snout is the shark's Achilles heel, the predator's most sensitive areas are really its eyes and its gills. Aiming for the nose, which shark experts say is not a particularly weak spot, is like using your hands to put out a fire.

'If you miss the snout the mouth is unfortunately close by,' noted R. Aiden Martin, a zoologist. 'It's not a good idea.'

Martin, an expert on shark behaviour and an avid diver, should know. He's logged more than fourteen thousand hours in the ocean with dozens of species of sharks and rays.

According to studies, most shark attacks can be divided into two groups. There are those by great whites, the Big Dog in the sea, which because of their size are particularly dangerous and known to attack without provocation. Then there are attacks by all other sharks, which often occur when the animals feel threatened – for instance, when a swimmer unknowingly wades into a feeding area near a school of fish.

But in both cases, the attacks are rarely deadly. Fewer than a hundred people worldwide are attacked by sharks and less than a third are killed. One study in the journal *Trauma* that looked at eighty-six consecutive attacks off the coast of South Africa found that 81 per cent of the victims suffered 'relatively minor injuries', whilst about 10 per cent were killed.

So if there's no easy way to fight off an attack, is there something you can do to keep a shark from noticing you if you happen on to the wrong side of the coral reef? Another bit of conventional wisdom holds that you should never wear anything too colourful in shark-infested waters, since sharks are supposedly attracted to bright colours. It's a notion that stems from studies years ago that followed groups of navy divers and found that those who wore bright flippers or anything else colourful along with their standard-issue wetsuits were more likely to be attacked or targeted.

But the reason has to do with contrast, not bright colours themselves. Like any predator, sharks look for prey with any features that separate them from the pack, a possible sign that the animal has an injury or abnormality that makes it more vulnerable. 'Sharks are very good at detecting these slight differences,' Martin explained.

They're so good, in fact, that a shark is unlikely to mistake a diver or swimmer for a seal, which is another widespread myth. When a great white shark attacks a seal, for example, it rushes towards the animal at about thirty miles an hour and smacks it out of the water with devastating force. When a shark approaches a swimmer, it does so slowly and deliberately.

But don't worry. You would never know it from the evening news, but the last thing you need to worry about at the beach this summer is a shark attack. The odds of drowning are far greater.

Do you have to wait forty-five minutes after a meal before swimming?

Think of all the hours people spend beside pools and lingering on beaches every summer, counting the minutes since their last meal to avoid violating the most fundamental rule of swimming: never hop in the water on a full stomach.

I've personally whiled away hours, kicking myself for not having the will to ignore my hunger and save my lunch for the walk or ride home. Only once did I manage to work up the nerve to cut the forty-five-minute wait down to thirty minutes. After getting in the water, I was fine. No problems, I thought, and through some miracle no cramps.

From that I realized that the old wives' tale was a myth: you don't have to wait forty-five minutes, I told myself, you have to wait thirty.

You've probably done some creative timekeeping of your own.

But when it comes down to it, you don't have to wait any time at all.

The theory behind this near universally accepted poolside wisdom is that the process of digestion increases blood flow to the stomach – away from the muscles needed for swimming – and leads to cramps, which can heighten the risk of drowning.

But while swimming strenuously on a full stomach could conceivably lead to cramps – it takes about four hours for the stomach to empty completely – for most recreational swimmers the chances are small. Even if you did get a cramp while swimming, how difficult would it be to climb out of the pool or head back to shore? No wonder that at least one study that looked at drownings found that fewer than 1 per cent occur after the victim has a meal.

Meals that include a drink or two of alcohol are another story. In 1989, a study in the US journal *Pediatrics* looked at almost a hundred adolescents who drowned and found that 25 per cent had been intoxicated. One year later, a study of hundreds of drowning deaths among adults in California found that 41 per cent were alcohol-related.

Perhaps all those poolside, swim-up bars at resorts and hotels aren't such a great idea after all.

Does walking in the rain keep you drier than running?

Caught in a downpour without an umbrella, most people pick up their pace. It is not a decision that should require much thought. But for decades people have been saying that a person who runs in the rain gets wetter.

When you run, more of your body is exposed to more droplets of water, the argument goes. Say you decide to break into a sprint – wouldn't you collide head-on with more droplets, making the front of your body even wetter? Most people would not consider this one of the enduring questions of modern science. But over the years, a small army of scientists has invested a surprisingly enormous amount of time and brainpower in debunking what should be a no-brainer, publishing study after study, some with convoluted titles like 'An Optimal Speed for Traversing a Constant Rain', and others that get right to the point, such as 'Is It Really Worth Running in the Rain?'

If anything, the research on this question demonstrates how scientists have an uncanny ability to take a simple question, dissect it relentlessly, overanalyze it and come up with a complicated answer – all for the sake of greater knowledge.

One of the first studies to examine this claim came to several conclusions, with the most important sounding like an ancient enigma: 'Maximizing the velocity through the rain will be rainstrike-minimizing.' Translation: spend less time in the rain, get less wet. The number of raindrops hitting you from above is not affected by velocity, but the number you run into is. In other words, you should run and lean forward.

Then, in 1987, an Italian physicist determined that if the distance is short enough, sprinting gets a person less wet than walking – but only by about 10 per cent. Translation: running isn't worth the effort. That finding was in line with the conclusion of another study conducted by a British researcher in 1995, which reported that it makes no difference whether a person walks or sprints, since the different variables cancel each other out.

But perhaps the final word on the subject came from two meteorologists at the National Climatic Data Centre in North Carolina, USA. Suspecting that earlier studies overestimated the average walking pace, they adjusted for certain variables: the effects of wind and the fact that runners tend to lean forward, shielding the front of their bodies, but exposing the back.

To put their findings to a practical test, the two researchers experimented on themselves. They waited for it to rain, then put on identical dry outfits that had been pre-weighed, and tucked plastic bags under their clothes to catch any water that might seep through. One decided he would walk, the other that he would run. Over a distance of 100 metres, or about 330 feet, they found that running in heavy rain kept them drier – by as much as 40 per cent.

That is a finding that for scientists was years in the making. But after I first wrote about this great mystery of our time, Jonathan Kaufman, a reader in New York, pointed out the obvious.

'The results of scientific studies seem to suggest, contrary to an old wives' tale, that running in the rain keeps a person somewhat drier than walking in the rain. I would agree, even though the most important aspect was overlooked: running means that you'll get out of the rain that much faster!'

Can cold weather really cause a cold?

What could be more miserable than a cold, dreary and bitter winter, except, of course, for the intolerable wave of aches, sniffles, sneezing and congestion that invariably comes along with it?

No wonder, then, that winter weather and its link to the common cold has been the stuff of medical lore for centuries. Throughout history, scientists have tried to get to the bottom of this old bromide, carrying out study after study and using legions of brave but shivering volunteers to find out whether anyone can really catch a cold from catching a chill.

Common wisdom says yes. If you are foolhardy enough to step outside in the dead of winter with wet hair, damp clothes or without the aid of warm layers, then Old Man Winter will almost certainly inflict his wrath upon you. Any mother or family doctor can tell you that.

But scientists have also insisted for centuries that the direct relationship between sickness and cold is an illusion, arguing that colds are more common in the winter only because the weather drives people indoors, where germs are given more chances to jump from one person to another.

To prove this theory and to debunk what seems like a link that to most of us is plain as day, researchers have gone to extraordinary and almost comical lengths. In the 1950s, one group recruited hundreds of adult subjects, exposed them to infected mucus, and then split them into two groups. One group sat in a sixty-degree room in their socks and underwear, while the other group – wrapped in winter clothing – was locked in a large freezer for a couple of hours. Days later, the scientists discovered that the subjects had all caught colds at exactly the same rate as the warm control group.

Through the years, other studies have tried to accomplish the same goal in similar ways, forcing volunteers exposed to infected mucus to wander around in cold environments wearing wet clothes, damp clothes, dry clothes or no clothes at all. Other studies have focused on people with wet hair; still others have forced people to sit at card tables in meat lockers to see whether it really is proximity that facilitates cold transmission.

Almost all of them reached the same conclusion: it's close quarters and hygiene, not temperature, that matter.

But a few decades ago, scientists discovered the most common cause of the common cold – the rhinovirus – and they began to look at its effects on the immune system. Could cold weather somehow weaken the immune system, making it easier for the rhinovirus to cause infection? As they studied the rhinovirus, they learned that, like many bugs, it thrives in humidity, and they discovered that it actually does most of its damage not in the winter, but in the spring and autumn, when the weather is wet and mild. That is also a time, like winter, when people are driven indoors to escape the sogginess outside.

With that new knowledge, scientists are now discovering that the answer to this question is not as clear-cut as it once seemed.

The tide has turned in favour of the old wives' tale, with research increasingly finding that a drop in body temperature can in fact bring on a cold. One carefully conducted study showed this in 2005 by having hundreds of unlucky volunteers keep their bare feet in icy water for long periods, while others kept dry. Within five days, 29 per cent of those in the cold group developed sore throats and runny noses, compared with less than 10 per cent in the second group.

The study was one of the most convincing to date. And it reinforces what many scientists say is now the prevailing wisdom: both theories on the increase in colds during cold weather are correct. People get more colds in the winter in part because nasty weather drives them inside, but also because frigid temperatures lower immunity, making you more susceptible to infection or exacerbating any dormant infection that you already have.

Either way, it's better to err on the side of staying warm.

Can arthritis be affected by changes in the weather?

We all know by now that chewing gum doesn't take seven years to pass through your digestive tract, and an apple a day isn't going to keep the doctor away. But surely all the thousands, if not millions, of people who say their arthritis waxes and wanes with the weather can't be wrong, right?

How could they be? It's a notion that dates all the way back to Hippocrates, the Father of Medicine, who coined the term 'arthritis' and wrote about its connection to the weather in 400 BC. Nowadays, many people with rheumatoid arthritis believe their condition fluctuates with changes in the weather; they say they can feel a storm coming in their bones.

Then again, Hippocrates also believed that people developed arthritis from eating too much food and that the condition was worsened by poisons in the body that needed to be drained. If you ask most scientists today, they'll insist that the weather has no influence on arthritis at all, or at least as much as the rain dance has on the rain.

The question of whether arthritis ebbs and flows with the weather is one of the most divisive in medical literature. Years of research have produced studies that are both conflicting and confusing. Some have found associations and some have not. Some have shown that pain increases when humidity or barometric pressure rises, while others have found that it decreases. Some have found that changes in weather affect arthritic pain instantly, while others say it takes a few days.

But most studies have found that there is no connection at all. One team of researchers followed eighteen people with arthritis for fifteen months and found no patterns between the levels of pain the subjects experienced each day and local weather reports. Another group tracked seventy-five rheumatoid arthritis patients, comparing their diary entries during a seventy-five-day period with local weather patterns, and did find that self-reported pain levels were highest on cold, overcast days and just after days with high barometric pressure. But overall the effect was not statistically significant.

Most scientists believe that the issue is a figment of human instinct, in particular the innate tendencies to look for patterns where there are none and to make up rules to explain random events. If your joints ache frequently and sporadically, you look for a reason, and it's easy to tie it to external events, these scientists say, especially when people have been doing so for centuries.

But not everyone buys this. Another strong possibility is that changes in the weather influence only inflammatory types of arthritis, such as rheumatoid arthritis, and that most studies have not found a relationship because they lump every type of arthritis together. When you consider that in rheumatoid arthritis the amount of lubricating fluid in the joints increases, it is not difficult to see how cooler temperatures and changes in barometric pressure might have an effect.

A large study published in the journal *Rheumatology* in 2002 showed just that: it found that people with rheumatoid arthritis were more likely to report an increase in pain on days with low temperatures, high atmospheric pressure and high humidity than people with osteoarthritis. Other studies have found similar patterns among people with various types of inflammatory disease.

Whenever I discuss this question, I'm reminded of something a woman wrote to me shortly after I first wrote about arthritis and the weather in 2004. The woman, Brenda Cummings, expressed a sentiment shared by many people.

'Why can't doctors and scientists simply believe what people say about their pain? It's the same as dismissing hormonal women as hysterical and not worthy of consideration.' She went on, 'It's interesting that in the very same issue of the paper there was an article about doctors' listening skills, or lack thereof. As someone with arthritis, I can say unequivocally that my condition is influenced by weather patterns, and no study will change my bottom line.'

Point well taken.

Do you lose most of your body heat through your head?

Put on a hat, my mother always said. It's the same warning parents everywhere give their children before sending them outside on bitter winter days. For many of us, it meant having our heads mummified with winter caps, earmuffs and scarves before we were allowed to step a foot outside the house.

Parents, God bless them, are known to dispense this advice with the best intentions. But the popular belief behind it, dare I say it, is misguided. Despite what many people have heard about half, most, two-thirds, or any other significant quantity of the body's heat escaping from the head on cold winter days, it is just not true.

Believe it or not, this is an old wives' tale that has its origins in military research. Dr Daniel I. Sessler, an expert on hypothermia who has investigated the myth, explained to me with some amusement that, about five decades ago, the military, for whatever reason, decided to conduct tests on body-heat loss by dressing people in Arctic survival suits and exposing them to frigid conditions. The short of it is that the suits only covered the subjects from the neck down, so naturally most of their body heat escaped through their heads, which no one at the time seemed to realize.

Sessler, a sharp, witty and bearded anaesthesiologist from a family of scientists, laughed as he pointed out the obvious: this was no fair comparison. If you did the same experiment with people dressed in wetsuits, only about 10 per cent of their heat loss would come from their heads.

The fact is that the amount of heat released by any part of your body depends in large part on its surface area. The greater the area, the more heat can escape. So on a cold day, you'll always lose more heat through an exposed arm or leg than you'll lose through your bare head.

There's another reason people believe that body heat escapes from the head. It's because studies have found that the face, the head and the upper chest area are up to five times as sensitive to changes in temperature as other parts of the body. This creates the illusion that covering up those areas traps in more heat, but in reality clothing another part of the body does just as much to reduce overall heat loss.

When it's cold outside, our bodies respond in several ways. The first is by constricting blood vessels in the arms and legs, which reduces blood flow to the extremities. This protects the brain and vital organs in the trunk of your body, but it leaves your fingers and your toes susceptible to frostbite. In effect, your body sacrifices these less-than-crucial digits. Another response to cold is shivering, which generates heat.

We also get goosebumps, though because of evolution these no longer have a very important function. Back in the days when humans had much more hair on their bodies, contracting the tiny muscles at the base of each hair would create a fluffy layer of insulation that helped retain body heat. Unlike other mammals, since we no longer have much hair on our bodies (well, most of us at least), this no longer works as well, and in the end we're just left with bumpy skin.

11
The Perfect Nightcap
Getting a good night's sleep

Sleep, as the British author Charles Caleb Colton once wrote, is a bundle of paradoxes. We go to it with reluctance, yet we quit it with regret. We make up our minds every night to end it early, but we make up our bodies every morning to continue it longer than we should.

Sleep may be one of the most basic human activities, but it is the subject of many puzzling questions, and perhaps the most mysterious question of all is also the most fundamental: why exactly do we need it?

Despite more than fifty years of intense research on the reasons, nature and mechanisms underlying sleep, no one to this day – not even the most brilliant scientist – can explain its core purpose. We spend a third of our lives unconscious. Shouldn't we know why?

In the annals of psychology, no other human behaviour – sex, language, desire – has resisted the scientific quest to dislodge its deepest secrets with as much tenacity as sleep.

Did sleep evolve as a way to protect animals, keeping them out of sight late at night, when predators are on the prowl? If that indeed is the case, then why instead of merely secluding ourselves for a few hours once a day do we find ourselves driven inexorably into a state in which our brains disengage? That would not seem always to serve an animal's best interests.

Do we sleep because we need rapid eye movement, or REM, stage sleep – the deep, restorative stage of sleep that consolidates morsels of knowledge so we can make room for new memories? That would seem to make a lot of sense from a scientific standpoint. But some forms of memory, such as rote or repetitive learning, are largely unaffected by sleep. And what are we to make of the four stages of sleep other than rapid eye movement, the ones that appear to play little role, if any, in consolidating memories? What purpose do they serve?

Perhaps our brains and bodies view sleep as a time to recover from the wear and tear of the daily grind, a time for our bodies to heal and grow in various ways. But this theory, too, has its problems. We know from studies that sleep deprivation has not been shown dramatically to alter our restorative processes nor does it slow the growth of our muscles and other organs.

So maybe after all these years, we should accept what our overdriven, sleep-deprived, stimulant-obsessed society seems to like as the simplest and most likely explanation for sleep: it is a symptom of caffeine deprivation.

No one can say for sure, at least not yet.

But while the answer to that most peculiar of questions about the human desire to wrap oneself in slumber once a day remains a mystery, thousands of studies have helped shed light on other questions about sleep that for the average person are just as puzzling. Many of the answers to those questions can drastically affect how we choose to go about our lives.

Vexing questions such as: is too much sleep bad for you? Do we need less sleep as we get older? Is yawning *really* contagious? And, of course, the question that faces all caffeine addicts: which has more, tea or coffee?

Which has more caffeine – tea or coffee?

Maybe it is a reflection of our constant struggle to ward off sleep, or simply the desire for that scintillating buzz that comes from a good cup of coffee. Worldwide, caffeine is the most popular drug, far ahead of nicotine and alcohol. Some anthropologists speculate that its use may even date as far back as the Stone Age.

Still, many people who start their day with either of the two most common sources of caffeine – coffee and tea – probably couldn't tell you with certainty which contains more. The confusion is not surprising. Pound for pound, experts say, tea has more caffeine than coffee. But while a pound of tea leaves often yields several hundred cups of tea, the same quantity of ground beans usually makes fewer than a hundred cups of coffee, making it a more potent pick-me-up.

Depending on the blend of tea leaves, the brand and the amount of brewing time, an eight-ounce cup of tea can contain anywhere from 20 to 90 milligrams of caffeine, while a similar serving of coffee varies from 60 to 180 milligrams. The longer your tea is brewed, the more caffeine it contains: tea brewed for one minute can contain as much as 35 milligrams per five ounces, while tea brewed for five minutes can contain as much as 50 milligrams per five ounces. Tea brewed for twenty or thirty minutes? Who has that much time on their hands anyway?

When it comes to coffee, fine ground beans brewed by the drip method produce the most caffeine. Percolated coffee has slightly less, and instant coffee contains the least. But a cup of either still has more caffeine than a twelve-ounce can of Coke, which contains about 45 milligrams.

Decaffeinated versions of both tea and coffee, meanwhile, have fewer than 5 milligrams of caffeine, which is about the same as an ounce of milk chocolate. Black tea and green tea are roughly equal. But most tea drinkers don't realize that tea has another strong stimulant besides caffeine, called theophylline. Although it is less potent than caffeine, in high enough doses it can rev up the central nervous system. A five-ounce cup of tea contains about 1 milligram of it.

For those determined souls who prefer their daily boost in tablet form, one pill of Vivarin or NoDoz (maximum strength) contains 200 milligrams of caffeine. But whatever your chosen method, decades of research have proven that no amount of caffeine in any form can conquer grogginess as well as a peaceful night's sleep.

Is too much sleep bad for you?

Most adults, let alone teenagers, relish the thought of unplugging the alarm and sleeping in late. We go to bed late, we wake up early and we spend our days drinking coffee, eating sugar, sipping Coke and chain-smoking cigarettes, all in an effort to amp us up so we can slog through the day just to start the cycle all over again a few hours later.

We are told that all this sleep deprivation eventually exacts a toll. It affects us physiologically, making us tired, stressed and overweight. And it affects those around us, making us cranky, lethargic, irritable and increasing our odds of causing accidents at work and on the motorway.

But imagine for a second that the reverse were true. Imagine if the eight hours of sleep that health officials have long recommended could actually do us harm. What if too much sleep, in fact, was far worse than too little?

That is exactly what scientists now suspect. Throw out your old notions of how much sleep is too much and how much sleep is too little. The world of sleep research was turned on its ear in

2002 when a study of more than a million adults discovered – after controlling for age, diet, smoking and other important variables – that getting more than seven hours of sleep a night is associated with a shorter lifespan.

The findings were shocking. In the six-year research period, the risk of dying climbed as people logged in more than seven hours of sleep. People who averaged eight hours a night had a 12 per cent increased chance of death and people who took sleeping pills were also more likely to die younger.

Six to seven hours of sleep a night seemed to be the magic dose conducive to a longer lifespan.

A single study with findings as unexpected as these can often be dismissed by an incredulous public as a fluke. But since its publication, several other studies have reached the same conclusion.

It has also been shown pretty clearly that life expectancy declines as sleep falls below seven hours, though not as steeply as it does with eight hours or more.

But the most interesting part about all this is that no one knows exactly why getting more than seven hours of shut-eye, in the long run, is so bad for your health. Oversleeping may be like overeating. We can eat more food than we need, drink more fluids than we need, indulge in sweets and alcohol, and all the while enjoy every second of it. But eventually we pay a price for this overindulgence, in the form of weight gain, disease and other health problems.

There may be some similar, unknown aspect of sleep that can also work against us. Then again, there is the strong possibility that too much sleep may not be the cause of sickness after all, but a result of it. People who sleep longer may simply have undiagnosed illnesses that cause fatigue – diabetes, sleep apnea, heart conditions – and earlier death. Most sleep experts are reluctant to draw firm conclusions just yet because the relationship between too much sleep and a shorter lifespan is still technically a correlation. Cause and effect has yet to be established.

In the meantime, it may be best to take the link at face value. Take it as your body's way of telling you to get your lazy self out of bed and enjoy the day.

Can sleep inspire creative thinking?

History suggests that a burst of creative inspiration, or even the solution to a baffling problem, can spring from the unconscious work of slumber.

Dmitri Mendeleev credited his discovery of the periodic table to a dream that showed him where to place the elements. Friedrich August Kekule discerned the ring shape of benzene in a somnolent vision of a snake biting its tail. And Otto Loewi, the Nobel laureate, said the idea for his landmark frog-heart experiment that proved the concept of chemical neurotransmission came to him in a dream.

Loewi famously woke up in the middle of the night to jot down his idea, then went to bed and woke up hours later, unable to make sense of his own handwriting. Only when he went to sleep the next night did the idea return to him in a second dream.

'This time I did not take any risk,' he later wrote. 'I got up immediately, went to the laboratory, made the experiment on the frog's heart, and at five o'clock the chemical transmission of nervous impulse was conclusively proved.'

Were these exceptional cases – mere flukes – or the most notable examples of sleep's ability to open the door to insight? Dismiss them if you choose. But the strongest explanation proffered by science is that sleep and dreams have powerful

effects on the organization and storage of memories that we're only now beginning to understand. Our ability to get to information stored in our memories – both consciously and unconsciously – is a crucial part of problem solving, and access to those memories is apparently where sleep comes in.

During sleep, the brain does a lot of heavy lifting. Memories are consolidated. Things that we've seen during the day are solidified into new memories. And information is moved from short-term storage to long-term storage, where it can be accessed later for the task at hand. Studies that examine patterns of brainwave activity during sleep and dreaming have hinted at this strongly, but it's also been illustrated in more direct ways.

One of the best examples was a 2004 study in the journal *Nature* that involved training several groups of students to perform a memory task. Each student learned two rules for converting a string of eight numbers into a new string of numbers, and each group was tested once after training and then again eight hours later. No one was told, though, that there was a third, hidden rule that could reduce the steps in the calculation, allowing the problem to be solved immediately.

Sixty per cent of the students who were allowed to sleep in the interval worked out the hidden rule. But only 22 per cent of those who stayed awake – some through the night, others through the day – discovered it.

At the same time, another group that slept for eight hours without being trained was never able to figure out the rule, suggesting that sleeping helped only if memories of the task were formed first. This last control condition also helped rule out the possibility that sleep deprivation or circadian rhythms accounted for the findings.

What the study demonstrated pretty nicely is that new memories are manipulated during sleep in a way that stimulates insight, which then seeps into consciousness. How this happens, or which brain regions are involved, is not yet known. Scientists have learned that explicit memory tasks are usually associated with deep stages of sleep. But anecdotal evidence suggests that insight is gleaned from dreams, which occur in the rapid eye movement, or REM, stage of sleep. It may be that both contribute to the process in different ways.

Whatever the mechanisms behind creative slumber, if a crucial exam is imminent, a big presentation looming, or a complicated problem weighing on your mind, it might be best to sleep on it.

Can exercising at night disrupt your sleep?

In these days when obesity rates are climbing and diseases linked to unhealthy lifestyles are soaring, we're being pounded with the exercise-whenever-possible message non-stop. Grab your dog and go for a midnight stroll. Join a gym with late hours. Just do whatever it takes to get your blood pumping before you hit the sack.

But when it comes to working out, the only thing that can be worse than not getting any exercise is suffering from a regimen that wrecks your sleep and keeps you up all night. Can a late-evening workout ever be *too* late?

As a general rule, most fitness *and* sleep experts say it's best to avoid intense physical activity in the immediate hours before bedtime, arguing that it takes at least three hours for adrenalin and other hormones that surge during exercise to return to normal levels. And perhaps the primary reason that sleep specialists are concerned about late exercise is that it can raise core body temperature, which needs to drop for healthy sleep.

But time and time again, examinations of the claim have failed to find that exercising before bed impairs sleep. One study published in the US journal *Physiology and Behavior* in 1998 had a group of students exercise moderately for about an hour on two separate nights, in one case ninety minutes before bedtime and in the other case thirty minutes before bedtime.

The activity, the researchers found, had no significant effects on the amount of time the subjects needed to fall asleep. Nor did it affect any other factors indicating how well they slept, including duration of sleep and their number of 'waking episodes' during the night. Several other studies have found the same.

One researcher who has published widely on the subject is Dr Shawn D. Youngstedt, a trim, athletic professor who admits to exercising at night and notes that he still manages to sleep 'just fine'. In fact, Youngstedt has found that exercise before bed can actually promote sleep by easing anxiety, tiring you out and making you more relaxed. His studies have also found that the rise in body temperature that was long thought to disrupt sleep might actually be beneficial, in part because the area of the brain that helps lower body temperature promotes sleep as well.

Youngstedt is part of a growing legion of scientists who say time of the day should never be a barrier to exercise. But it's also clear that, as with any fitness routine, there is individual variation. Some people will work out before bedtime and sleep just fine. Others might find their bodies don't respond as well. People who feel that exercise in the post-dinner hours disrupts their sleep should listen to their bodies, not to the science, and adjust their workout schedules accordingly.

Does melatonin really help you beat jet lag?

Some bleary-eyed travellers will do anything to conquer jet lag. I once had a friend who flew to meetings in other countries several times a month and popped nearly every imaginable aid for overcoming sleepless nights and chronic jet lag – coffee, caffeine pills, sleeping pills, amphetamines, energy drinks, even prescription drugs. But nothing worked without making her shaky and nervous, she discovered, and every day was a struggle to stay awake.

Then she turned to melatonin, the legendary hormone that in humans regulates the sleep-wake cycle. But to no avail. Like many people who try melatonin, she found it no different than the previous pills – in a word, useless. That did not come as a shock to me. People have been taking melatonin for decades and, by and large, the millions who have tried it remain deeply divided. Some say it has no value; others swear by it.

But the story behind melatonin is more complicated than that, as reams of studies show. I can't think of another over-the-counter pill designed to beat sleepiness that has been studied more, and yet the medical literature remains conflicting and confused.

Dozens of studies have tried to determine whether melatonin can ease symptoms of jet lag, with some finding that it helps in small doses, and others concluding it's no better than a placebo. But it turns out that most of those studies shared one big problem: they did not account for the little annoyances involved in flying, which affect us all differently and in many ways are separate from jet lag.

Taking melatonin has been shown to help reset body rhythms, but it cannot alleviate the symptoms of jet lag that result from the stress of travelling itself – sprinting through busy airports, dealing with security, a shoddy diet, sudden weather changes, the prospect of meeting new business clients. All of these contribute in no small way to exhaustion and sleep disturbances.

One of the many scientists who have studied this topic and come away slightly dismayed is Dr Michael Terman, a sleep expert at the New York State Psychiatric Institute. Terman explained that the real problem is confusion over how jet lag is defined.

'We cannot say that all of the symptoms of jet lag are unequivocally due to circadian rhythm shifting,' Terman observed. 'We see for example that some people travelling long distances barely complain of jet lag, even though their internal clocks are undergoing marked change.'

But a consensus is emerging. Despite individual differences, there is one technique for eliminating jet lag that most studies, as well as the researchers I interviewed, bestow with a nod of approval. It is based on the fact that melatonin, unlike caffeine or nicotine, is a slow-acting hormone, not a stimulant. It will not wake you up or put you to sleep. And you can't simply pop it on the plane and expect it to kick in. You have to take it in advance for it to reset your body clock in time.

Let's say you're taking a flight from New York to Paris. The technique calls for you to start by taking small doses of melatonin for at least three days before your departure, while at the same time adjusting your sleep schedule by going to bed about an hour earlier each day. Then, approximately six hours after arriving in France, take in plenty of bright light, whether it's natural sunlight outdoors or artificial light in the hotel room.

If that does not work, do not despair. By mid-2008, jet lag may not even exist. According to published reports, some airlines are experimenting with new ways to help their passengers reach their destinations feeling brand new.

Boeing, for example, is designing planes that can overcome the lighting, pressure, humidity and air quality problems that are the underlying causes of jet lag. Their planes will have electronically dimmable windows, lighting systems that can mimic the colours of a sunrise, more humidity, enormous windows that allow passengers in the middle seats to look outside and filtration systems that eliminate compounds and odours that heighten fatigue. The planes will also maintain lower onboard pressures to help give passengers about 10 per cent more oxygen, making them less tired.

All of this to conquer jet lag. Now if they could just do something about that awful airline food.

Do you need less sleep as you get older?

A comedian once said that as we age our lives come full circle. The older we get, the closer we get to infancy. By the time we reach our final years, we are cranky, complaining all the time, eating soft food because we have no teeth, and are constantly tired.

You could say the same is true when it comes to sleep. Infants nap frequently and sleep five hours a night, not unlike many seniors. It's well known that older people are typically early to bed, early to rise, and studies show that the average person spends about two fewer hours in bed each night aged seventy than they did aged thirty.

Conventional wisdom is that older people just don't need it. Sleep may not exactly be a waste of time, as Thomas Edison once described it, but as we get older, it seems, we require less and less of it – or so it was once thought.

While it may appear that the natural urge to rest somehow grows weaker with age, research on sleep suggests that is not the case.

What happens instead is that the composition of sleep changes, as people gradually spend less and less time in the deep, restorative stages of sleep. The duration of the REM phase, the stage in which we dream and our muscles relax most completely, diminishes markedly with age, as do the phases of sleep that are the deepest and most refreshing, stages 3 and 4. In people who are older than ninety, in fact, stages 3 and 4 may even disappear for good.

In the meantime, stage 1 of the sleep cycle, the phase that constitutes light sleep, increases. That means there's a greater likelihood of being easily awakened by noise or something as minor as the person lying next to you rolling over. The elderly are also more likely to have their sleep disturbed by pain, chronic illness, drug side effects, the need to use the bathroom or some other physiological discomfort.

All of which means that a typical night of sleep for the average older person is abbreviated and full of disruptions. As a result, they end up with fewer hours of sleep each night – and subsequently a need to make up for that loss during the day. And so the cycle continues.

One study published in the *Journal of the American Geriatric Society* in 1992, for example, compared a group of forty-five healthy people older than seventy-eight with thirty-three healthy adults aged twenty to thirty. It found that in a typical night, the older group experienced more waking episodes, more disordered breathing and more periodic movements than the younger group. They were also more likely to need a nap during the day to function properly, the study found, and those who took the most naps were also those who experienced the most interruptions in their sleep at night.

So it's not that we don't require as much sleep as we grow older so much as we just can't get enough of it at night, when it counts. Even with retirement and much more time to ourselves, getting a solid six or seven hours of sleep each night becomes a struggle. So enjoy your sleep now, because one day it'll be far more elusive.

Does the tryptophan in turkey really make you drowsy?

Who hasn't heard of the sleep-inducing effects of a hearty Christmas dinner? Turkey, popular wisdom holds, is filled with tryptophan, an amino acid that, as a precursor to the brain chemical serotonin, plays a role in sleep.

It's the reason we all slink over to the sofa and feel the urge to pass out after Christmas dinner. That, of course, and the strong desire to escape the relatives, the pile of dishes and those dreadful films that are played over and over all day long. After most Christmas dinners, I want nothing more than an antacid and a long nap.

But don't believe the old wives' tale about the soporific power of a turkey dinner. When you take a hard look at the science, this long-lived claim falls more into fiction than into fact.

Turkey is indeed a source of L-tryptophan, a natural sedative. But it's not that simple. To have any noticeable effect on the brain, tryptophan must be consumed by itself and on an empty stomach. When other amino acids and nutrients are present, tryptophan ends up fighting – largely unsuccessfully – to get across the blood-brain barrier. The more protein a meal contains, the harder it is for tryptophan to complete its journey to the brain.

But in the presence of mostly carbohydrates, the hurdles are fewer. Carbohydrates stimulate the pancreas to release insulin. This causes other amino acids to exit the bloodstream and frees up room for tryptophan, allowing it more opportunities to be converted into serotonin, the chemical that ultimately sedates you.

Keep in mind that turkey is not the only thing we eat that contains tryptophan. The chemical is found in a wide variety of foods – chicken, ground beef, beans – in similar amounts as turkey. It is also found in milk and other dairy products – the root of the notion that a glass of warm milk can conquer insomnia.

To get some more meaty facts, I called up Dr Stasia J. Wieber, the director of the Centre for Sleep Medicine at Mount Sinai Medical Centre in Manhattan. Wieber responded knowingly when I posed the question and said she hears it all the time. She too has had to debunk it, explaining to people that the reason we fall into a stupor on a stomach full of turkey is plain and simple overeating, not the miracle of tryptophan.

Think about all the fat we eat at Christmas – the stuffing, the sausages, the pork pie, the mince pies, the Christmas pudding – which requires a great deal of energy to digest. This forces the body to redirect blood flow toward the abdomen and away from other organs. Then, there's the added sleep-inducing effect of any alcohol in the two or three drinks you've had.

As for the sedative effect of a glass of warm milk, the science is hazy; its effects may be psychological.

'For many people, a glass of warm milk is part of a routine, like putting on your pyjamas, that signals to your body that you're getting ready for bed,' Wieber told me.

Ah, the placebo effect. It must be true. Just thinking about all this is making me drowsy.

Can a nightcap help you sleep?

A century ago, it was common in many countries for people to don soft, fuzzy caps before crawling into bed. The comfy hats locked in warmth and aided sleep.

But nowadays, nightcaps tend to come in the form of a glass of whisky or two, and plenty of people are convinced that alcohol is a great antidote to the occasional bout of insomnia. But while a drink before bed can help you drift off more quickly, in the long run, it'll most likely lead to tossing and turning throughout the night.

That's because, after inducing a brief period of increased arousal, alcohol, a central nervous system depressant, causes sedation. It is this calming effect that helps you doze off, whether in bed, on a friend's couch or, after a night of heavy drinking in college, on your knees with your head in the toilet.

A few hours later, though, the alcohol starts to interfere with sleep and can lead to middle-of-the-night insomnia. The most likely scenario is a night of poor sleep, less deep sleep, and the compulsion to wake up earlier than usual, making you feel as if you didn't get enough sleep.

One study in 2002 found that just one drink before bed can disrupt activity in a part of the brain called the thalamus, subsequently leading to wakefulness. An earlier study in 1993 showed that moderate alcohol consumption in the evening could cause the symptoms of obstructive sleep apnea – a narrowing or blockage of the airways – in people with no previous sleep disorder. A drink before bed can worsen existing sleep conditions as well.

Interestingly, studies show that about half of all alcoholics have sleep problems long before they start drinking, compared to only about 10 to 15 per cent of the general population. No one is suggesting that sleep disorders lead to alcohol dependence, but it suggests that there may be some minor relationship.

Perhaps more importantly, alcohol, as most people know, also induces snoring – which can make a peaceful night of sleep more elusive both for you and the person lying next to you.

Is yawning contagious?

Prepare to yawn uncontrollably. Don't worry. That statement is not a direct commentary on what you are about to read.

As most people may have noticed, yawning can have such a strong and immediate impact that merely reading about it, thinking about it, or hearing someone else do it is enough to make us yawn. You can even set up your own little office experiment to confirm it. Sit at your desk at about 2 p.m. and observe the rippling chain reaction that one person's post-lunch-slump-induced yawn can trigger.

And it's a behaviour that is not limited to us jaded modern types. Yawning is a mysterious act with ancient origins, one that can be seen in a diverse cross section of the animal kingdom

– fish, crocodiles, primates, dogs, even birds. Yawning has even been observed in newborn babies and human foetuses.

So, surprisingly, yawning is contagious.

But the issue is not exactly black and white. In a series of good old scientific experiments, researchers found that it's generally people who score high on tests of self-awareness and empathy that fall prey to the contagiousness of yawning. That, they found, applies to about 50 per cent of the population.

But on to the other 50 per cent of the population. Studies show that people who don't find yawning contagious are more likely to have problems with self-recognition, an extreme example of which condition is schizophrenia. These are people who also score low on tests of empathy.

Animals can be infected by the yawn bug too. One study by researchers at the University of Stirling in Scotland found that a third of adult chimps exposed to videos of yawning chimps will end up yawning themselves.

But one thing no one can say for sure is why anyone – man, woman, or chimp – yawns to begin with. Conventional wisdom suggests that we yawn when we are bored. That's one reason. But scientists say they have also observed yawning in professional athletes just before a big event, in entertainers before they go on stage and in dogs getting ready to pounce on one another.

The more scientifically-minded argue that we yawn when we have a shortage of oxygen in the blood or a build-up of carbon dioxide in our systems. That deep breath and gaping of the mouth that characterize yawning supposedly counteract this. But studies have also found that breathing high levels of carbon dioxide does not trigger yawning, nor does breathing high levels of oxygen inhibit it.

OK, you say, but how about sleepiness? Clearly sleepiness must be the underlying cause of yawning, right? Not exactly. While research confirms that people really do yawn when they are sleepy – obviously – it also shows that we yawn the most in the hour after we wake up, even after a long, sufficient night of sleep.

Rest assured, though, that there are more than enough scientists working on this one to ensure that one day the mystery of yawning will be unravelled, if indeed there is a mystery there at all.

Epilogue
This wacky planet, Earth

It is blamed for sudden surges in crime, suicide, mental illness, fertility and dogs howling in the street. It has influenced the way some people buy and sell their stock and convinced others that their occasional bouts of restlessness have nothing to do with how much television they watch or coffee they drink.

The notion that a full moon spurs odd behaviour has been around for centuries. Ancient cultures looked upon the moon as a sign of fertility and since Roman times people have blamed full moons for all sorts of oddball antics, hence the word 'lunacy', from the Latin word for moon.

In the last few decades, all sorts of scientists – gynaecologists, epidemiologists, psychologists and even a dentist – have set out to sort through the truth of this ancient legend. Turns out that as mysterious and alluring as the crazy moon may seem, it is more romance than reality.

But along the way, the studies proposed have been almost as quirky as the myth itself. One study looked at workplace data and found that rates of absenteeism were actually lower on days with full moons than on other days. Another study in 1982 blamed full moons and new moons for sharp increases in traffic accidents – until it was revealed later that the researchers had been studying full and new moons that fell on weekends, which is a time when traffic accidents are always more likely.

Still another study, which appeared much earlier in the *New England Journal of Medicine*, looked at thousands of births across fifty-one lunar cycles and found that there was no predictable influence on deliveries or birth complications at all. What scientists discovered is that most childbirths occur later in the week, largely because many women prefer having labour induced before the weekend, full moon or not.

Other studies have tried to link full moons to increased calls to poison centres, higher rates of suicide attempts, more admissions to psychiatric hospitals and upsurges in homicide rates. But for every one of those studies claiming a link, it seems, there is another more rigorous study contradicting it.

Let's think about the direct effect a full moon has on the Earth for a second. Both the moon and the sun exert gravitational forces on the planet. When they're both on one side, known as the new-moon phase, their gravitational forces tug on the oceans, creating the tides. When they're on either side of us, the full-moon phase, their gravitational forces work against each other.

Since most people argue that the gravitational forces of the moon act on us because we're 80 per cent water, in essence like a human tidal effect, it would actually make more sense for the new moon, if anything, to have strange effects on us. The other problem is that the moon's weak gravitational pull is only noticeable in the oceans and in coastal areas, where the scale is much greater. The truth is, the moon's gravitational tug on humans is infinitely small – millions of times weaker than the force you are exerting on this book.

Another theory suggests that the full-moon effect has more to do with moonlight than gravitational alterations. But it seems hard to believe that a little extra moonlight would drive hordes of people insane, inspire criminals or set off labour contractions.

But just to be sure, a group of scientists prepared an extensive report in 1996 that examined over a hundred studies on lunar effects. This meta-analysis found no relationship between any cycle of the moon and baby births, traffic accidents, crime, major disasters or a dozen other things typically associated with the moon.

About the only behaviour full moons really seem to affect is that of scientists: it gives them a reason, like all the other old wives' tales, common cures, urban legends, long-time myths, modern fears and hopeful bromides in *Don't Go to Work on Mondays*, to design silly studies.

Acknowledgements

I am indebted to the countless researchers whose studies of scientific matters both quirky and serious provided me with ample material for this book. I also owe a debt to the many fans of the 'Really?' column in *The New York Times*, who over the past few years have supplied me with a wealth of intriguing questions to explore.

The column itself would not have been possible without the creative genius of my editor at *Science Times*, Erica Goode, who got the column off the ground and guided it along as it snowballed into a book. Friends and loved ones of mine – Garren, Dave, Marisa and Steve, to name a few – were constant sources of ideas and support as well.

I am grateful to Alex Ward, the director of book development at the *Times*, for his time and dedication to the project, and to Robin Dennis, my editor at Times Books, whose careful edits and fantastic input made the book tremendously better. Thanks as well to Susan Edgerley, Joe Sexton, Chris Conway and Jodi Rudoren, my bosses at the *Times*, for allowing me – graciously – to take time away from my duties at the paper. My agents, Christy Fletcher and Emma Parry, get a big thanks for their efforts on my behalf. And my gratitude also goes to David Woodroffe, whose excellent illustrations grace this book, and to Jody Emery, the initial illustrator of the column.

Thanks as well to Arthur Gelb, Soma Golden Behr, Laura Chang, and everyone else at *The New York Times*, an amazing newspaper that has become a second family to me.